Adventures *in* Idealism

Adventures *in* Idealism

A Personal Record of the Life of Professor Sabsovich

By
Katharine Sabsovich

New York
Privately Printed for the Author
1922

Republished for the
Alliance Heritage Center
and the South Jersey Culture & History Center
2021

Initial Publication
Copyright, 1922
By Katharine Sabsovich

Room 1715
80 Maiden Lane
New York

Stratford Press, Inc.—American Bookbindery
New York, N. Y., U. S. A.

∾

Republished in 2021 for the Alliance Heritage Center
by the South Jersey Culture & History Center
Stockton University

Stockton University
101 Vera King Farris Dr., Galloway, NJ, 08205

stockton.edu/alliance-heritage/
stockton.edu/sjchc/

Additional material, foreword, afterword, and design Copyright
© 2021 by the South Jersey Culture & History Center.

ISBN-13: 978-1-947889-06-4

The South Jersey Culture & History Center received a project
grant from the New Jersey Historical Commission, a division of
the Department of State, which helped defray the costs of printing
this title.

"*To live in mankind is far more than to live in a name*"

Vachel Lindsay

Contents

From Those Who Knew Him Best

List of Illustrations

Additional Illustrations, new to this edition

NEW FOREWORD

IDEAL, Answering to one's highest conception, perfect; visionary of Platonic ideas.

Katherine Sabsovich, married to Hirsch Loeb Sabsovich (1860–1915) for thirty-three years, took pen in hand some six years after his death to record her memory of his greatness of spirit. In her description of Sabsovich, the man, she wrote that his "sincere and loving spirit lighted his every action."

Born in Berdiansk, Russia, young Sabsovich's father died when he was four years old. The next to youngest of seven siblings, young Grisha, as he was called, was an outstanding student. By the time he was ten he began earning wages as a tutor to help support the family. Education became a driving force in his early life which eventually developed into his career as Professor Sabsovich.

The onset of the terrorist pogroms against the Jews in Russia in 1881 increased a movement toward immigration to the United States organized by the "Am-Ohlom" movement. One of the purposes of Am-

Ohlom was to show the world that a Jew was able to become a productive worker if given the opportunity. The chief objective became the agricultural colonization movement. Sabsovich declared agriculture as his profession and became a leader in the "Back to the Land" movement, helping Jews to Farm in new lands.

Professor and Mrs. Sabsovich sailed for America in 1887, accompanied by their two young daughters. After a brief encounter with life in the large city of New York and an even shorter stay in Pittsfield, Massachusetts, Sabsovich was summoned to Fort Collins, Colorado, to assist the director of the Fort Collins Agricultural Experiment Station. Two years and a third child later found the family leading a comfortable and active life living on the campus of Fort Collins. However, the "Back to the Land" dream was still the focus of his aspirations.

In May 1890, those dreams became reality. The Baron de Hirsch Fund chose Professor Sabsovich to manage the proposed new Jewish Colony that would become Woodbine, located in Southern New Jersey. The Woodbine Tract was bought on August 11, 1891.

Sabsovich and twelve "pioneer farmers" arrived in Woodbine to find nothing but a railroad station, one house and a shanty. Everything was surrounded by thick woods. The men were not experienced in the hard labor before them so wood choppers from the small village of Dennisville three miles away were hired to work along with the future Jewish farmers. By the end of 1891, there were sixty men clearing the forest, building the planned sixty houses and creating a livable village.

Realizing that it might take several years to produce successful farms, the Baron De Hirsch Fund Committee sought out manufacturers to move their plants from the city to the wide-open spaces in Woodbine, New Jersey. The first clothing factory opened in 1892. The first schoolhouse was built at one end of town. The first kindergarten to open in Cape May County was started and yet another school was built in the center of town.

Americanization was critically important to Professor Sabsovich. Since the colonists came from mostly undemocratic forms of government, he wanted them to appreciate and enjoy the freedoms celebrated here in America. Every holiday, from Lincoln's birthday to the Fourth of July, was a special day in Woodbine. Flags and parades and large public gatherings were annual events. Special guest speakers from New York and Philadelphia were invited to Woodbine on these dates.

In 1894 Professor Sabsovich realized his dream to open an agricultural school. The Baron de Hirsch Agricultural School was established in Woodbine, New Jersey. The institution was the first secondary agricultural school in New Jersey. Although he spent twenty-five years devoted to the agricultural movement of the Jewish people and was hailed as a pioneer and innovator in the field, Professor Sabsovich did not live to experience the wide success of his efforts.

He left an indelible mark on the world of science, agriculture, philanthropy and his Jewish brethren.

Loved by his students and revered by the business and professional men and women he worked with, his beautiful spirit has left everyone a better person for knowing him.

> Jane Stark
> Executive Director
> Sam Azeez Museum
> of Woodbine Heritage
> of Stockton University

FOREWORD

Professor H. L. Sabsovich is recognized as one of the foremost figures in the field of Jewish social service. As a great part of his active life was given to the work of the Baron de Hirsch Fund, I consider it a privilege to make this acknowledgment for my colleagues and myself to his worth, his merit, and his undoubted achievements, as well as to his excellent administrative abilities, as the Builder of Woodbine and as the head of one of the Fund's most important institutions, the Woodbine Agricultural School, and later as General Agent for the Baron de Hirsch Fund.

He was a very exceptional man, in so far that he combined practical knowledge in very many directions and good executive capacity, together with an idealism as to the coming achievements of the Jewish immigrants, and the part they would fill in American life. It is gratifying to remember that he lived to see most of these prognostications come true. At all times he had the full confidence of the Trustees of the Fund, who relied upon his integrity of purpose, breadth of viewpoint and capacity to carry out a given program.

Nothing can be added to the simple and sympathetic record written by his devoted wife and to the excellent appreciation written by his associate, Mr. B. A. Palitz, except to say that he commanded respect, affection, and a high measure of appreciation from all those who had occasion to meet him in everyday life. Never a well man, his health was a great handicap, but still he sacrificed himself and never allowed his physical condition to interfere with his work. His death was felt by all the Trustees as a great loss to the cause which we were all attempting to serve, and every Trustee in addition felt a personal loss was sustained in taking away from us a man with whom we had always worked in complete harmony and sympathy.

Eugene S. Benjamin
October 20, 1921

CHAPTER I
SCHOOL DAYS IN RUSSIA

The man to whom I was happily married for thir-ty-three years is now some six years dead and buried in body, but not in spirit, not in deeds. It has taken me all of these six years to reach the point where I can speak of him with any degree of calmness—of his character, his work! His wonderful gentleness and kindness of heart; his fine, even severe sense of duty to his family, his friends, or to the cause in which he chanced to be interested, made him beloved by all who knew him. And he always had some big cause to work for. In all the thirty-five years I knew him I do not remember a stretch of time when he was not actively engaged in some task of a public character. Since his death I have strongly felt that a life has gone out so stimulating to the youth of today and tomorrow—invaluable from whatever angle it may be considered—that, poorly as I may, I have decided to note down some of the things I know of him.

In September 1881, I met my husband at the home of a dear friend of mine. He was a tall man, very slim—all legs and arms it seemed—with a small, pale face, illumined by large, clear, gray-blue eyes; the features finely cut, and the nobly shaped head surmounted by thick brown curls. Though only twenty years of age he looked older, because of the small beard so commonly worn by students in Russia then. He had just entered upon his second year in the Law School of the Odessa University, where a brilliant career was predicted for him.

It is to his younger sister that I am indebted for most of what I know of his childhood and boyhood. He was born in Berdiansk, Russia, an Azov seaport. His father died when he was not quite four years old, leaving his mother with seven children—four boys and three girls. My husband was next to the youngest, and his sister, the baby of the family, was only one and a half years old. The two eldest boys, big men of fourteen and twelve, now became the sole support of the family. While nothing more could be expected of Grisha, as they called my husband, than that he should remain in the Talmud Torah, or Hebrew School, he was there distinguishing himself as the brightest pupil. In fact, by the time he was eight his brothers were so well pleased with his unusual ability and his love of study that they decided he must enter the Gymnasium just then opening its doors in Berdiansk. Though my husband was generally known to his Russian friends as Grisha or Gregory, he later in life used only the initials H. L., signifying Hirsch Loeb, the names formally given him by his parents.

Grisha was one of the first recommended for the free scholarships which the gymnasium was offering to the best pupils of the different schools. The scholarship consisted of free tuition and free books. It meant that he would have to be supported, but though the family had to battle with great hardships, it was decided that Grisha should continue his studies.

From the first year to the very last Grisha was at the head of his classes. But the gold medal which was rightfully his he forfeited. It happened in this way: During the last year at the Gymnasium one of the teachers, who was greatly admired by the pupils, was dismissed for expressing a little more liberalism than was wanted. The pupils refused to return to the classroom unless this teacher was reinstated. As a result of his participation in this protest my husband lost the right to the gold medal.

By the time he was ten he had begun to earn his living as a teacher, coaching the more prosperous classmates, and preparing others for their entrance examinations. To be sure, the pay was a mere pittance, but he was the pride of the family and the talk of the town for earning it at so early an age. Money, however, did not mean much to him. He was exceedingly kindhearted, and he was always giving lessons gratis to his less fortunate friends, especially during examination time.

"And so," writes his sister, "he worked very hard and had very little time for play. But one great temptation he had, and that was flying kites. Whenever I was fortunate enough to get one, I knew Grisha would join me and leave his books for that sport."

He was a great reader. Every moment he could spare from his lessons and coaching, he spent in reading. When we wanted to find Grisha we had only to look to Mother's bed, and there he was, hidden in the big feather mattress and pillows, cuddled in fairyland, deep in his book.

Vacation time would come, but he was still the busiest boy, for then he had to prepare pupils for entrance examinations, and to coach those who had failed in the examinations at the end of the year. So altogether he worked hard. Every year he contributed more and more toward the support of the family and with the best will in the world. He was so grateful to his elder brothers for giving him the chance that they had missed that he felt he could never do enough for them.

So it was that working hard, denying himself that essential pleasure of childhood play, he caught a severe cold. Inflammation settled on his lungs, and at one time we thought that we should lose him. But at last, the danger over, Grisha appeared among his schoolmates once more, a very emaciated little boy. He really looked as though he had been in the grip of death. He was so thin, that I, his younger sister, carried him in my arms. I remember though that shortly after his illness he suddenly began to grow and soon shot up into a tall, lank youth.

It proves how high he stood in the opinion of his teachers that although he had been sick during examination time, he was promoted to the fifth class of the Gymnasium without the test and with high honors.

In his eighth year of school a number of pupils at the Odessa Gymnasium were expelled for being mixed up in some Workingmen's Circles and liberal propaganda work, and had to forfeit their diplomas. They applied to the Berdiansk Gymnasium and were admitted. When they came to Berdiansk, two of them became boarders at the house of Grisha's mother. Those two boys became widely known in later years, Kostia Puritz as a physician, and Lyova Albert as a great social worker. All three became very close friends. The boys from the big city exercised a great influence on the country boy and quickened his interest in matters of public welfare. They had lived in the midst of the great movements of the time. They were full of big ideas and took a great interest in the newly started, revolutionary, underground paper, "Land and Freedom," which advocated the taking of the land by those who till it, and freedom of thought for all.

Berdiansk was a small country place, in no way to be compared with Odessa, but the three boys were not cast down. They set about organizing several "self-educational clubs," each taking the lead in a club where young men and women could come together and discuss affairs of general interest. That was in 1879, a time of great activity in all Russian revolutionary circles. Among these young idealists there was no question at the time of Jew and Christian,—all worked together in the cause hand in hand, organizing clubs for the masses. Of course these meetings were kept secret.

In May Grisha and his two chums graduated from the Gymnasium, and Puritz and Albert left for Odessa to enter law school. Grisha followed them in August. To enable him to pursue his studies his two Odessa friends, well known there, secured pupils for him in advance. So, when he arrived in the city, he found that he would have about seventy-five rubles a month, which would enable him to support, not only himself, but his younger sister. He therefore brought her from Berdiansk, secured lodgings and began to prepare her for college entrance.

This was the year that I graduated from Filler's Gymnasium. As soon as we were out of school four of the other graduates and I felt the need of doing something in an educational way for the Jewish poor. We decided to open a free school for Jewish girls who were not able to pay the fee to attend the private schools. Jewish girls were not admitted to the few elementary free schools of Russia. And yet we felt that these children, being of the poorest class—their families living in cellars and sub-cellars—needed a vocational as well as an elementary education. So we decided to open an elementary and vocational school for the girls, similar to the one opened a year previously for poor Jewish boys. Two of us were delegates to meet representatives of the Boys' School. One of these men was my husband.

He often came to our meetings to discuss ways and means, and so energetic was the spirit of these gatherings that in a few months we opened the school for Jewish girls with seventy-five children. The school is now known all over Russia as the "Anna Siegal School." Officially the school had to be run as a private one, because it was conducted without recognition from the government. Funds for running it had to be collected secretly, and the money was raised by holding balls, bazaars, and similar entertainments. The two schools were a nucleus for the development of similar schools for boys and girls which sprang up all through the Jewish quarter. To the best of my knowledge, the original two schools exist today, greatly enlarged and extended, and now supported openly by the various Jewish organizations and city funds.

My husband and I met frequently at the organizing conferences. Strong mutual interest ripened our friendship, and a year later, in the spring of 1881, we were formally betrothed.

CHAPTER II
ODESSA AND THE POGROM

The spring of 1881 was the most significant, the most interesting year in my husband's early life. He peacefully devoted himself to his studies, to his tutoring, to forming "Self-Education Centers," helping in the distribution of underground literature and establishing new centers. My husband counted among his friends as many Christians as Jews, and visited as many Christian homes as Jewish. The question of race and creed did not exist among the Intelligentzia at all. In the University the Jewish and Christian students were on the friendliest of terms. The meetings were just of one body—the student body. The good of Russia, of its working masses, of its peasants—these were the topics that interested and united the best among its members.

The autumn of 1881 changed everything. The whole spirit of the country was altered. The Terrorist Movement was then at its height, one high official after another having been assassinated. Czar Alexander II himself, was killed. The government needed an excuse, an explanation, a scapegoat for all the terror that was raging; for all the panic spread by the thick net of secret organizations. It was not difficult to find that scapegoat. Among the many, many Terrorists it was but natural that there should be a proportionate quota of Jews. The press, subsidized by the government, began a systematic hounding of the Jews, and denounced them as "the cause of all the trouble, inciting the people to riot and bloodshed." This cry found its echo in the universities. The Jewish students began to feel a change in atmosphere. They began to feel the animosity, not only of the Christian students, but of some of the professors as well. It was not enough to hear talk of Pogroms on the streets, in the cafes, in the places of amusement; it finally entered the university, too. A great many of the Christian students, organized in a body "to help kill the Jews." The Jewish students, to their bewilderment and sorrow, discovered the existence of the organized body and its terrible aim. All this made a lasting impression on my husband.

Some of the Jewish students called an indignation meeting, and a "Self-Defense League" was organized. Its purpose was to protect the Jewish populace during the Pogroms, which everyone knew would take place during the Passover holidays. Ten of the ablest young Jews in the student body took the lead, my husband being one of them. At once they began to organize the Jewish butchers, grain shovelers, bricklayers, and other young workers of strength and courage. They supplied every one with any kind of tool or weapon of defense they could lay hands on, and they assigned groups of the volunteers to places in the poorest and most crowded districts of the city where they expected the Czar's mercenaries to do their worst—and where, on account of their extreme poverty, the victims could not buy police protection after the manner of the more wealthy Jewish citizens.

And one Sunday afternoon—the fifth day of Passover and the first of Easter—while my husband was visiting me, the Pogrom broke out. We heard shrill whistling, the smashing of windows, the wild clamor of the hoodlums, and, above all, the shouts: "Kill! Kill the Jews!" My husband rushed out of the house, and that was the last I saw of him until three days later I visited him in the Odessa prison. He and his fellow students were nursing the wounds they had received from the hoodlums, while they were trying to protect the homes that had been attacked by the ruffians. The police had been out the whole first day of the massacre defending the hoodlums. They had clashed with the organized "Self-Defense" in several sections of the city, and bloody fights had taken place between the Pogromschiki and the Jewish defenders. The police, in their righteous anger, arrested every one of the young Jewish students and flung them into jail.

Despite the pressure brought to bear by the fathers of the students, a number of whom were wealthy and influential citizens, it was at least two weeks before their trial took place; and then it turned out to be a farce, for every one of the arrested men was released.

It is interesting to note that most of these young students of the "Self-Defense League" became in after years well-known scientists and social workers. Alexander Krasilchek, the widely known entomologist; Vladimir Chavkin, the bacteriologist; Kalmenowitz, who became later a member of the first Russian Duma; the respected physician, Kostia Puritz; and Lyova Albert, lawyer, the same youth with whom my husband became so friendly in Berdiansk. Of the last named, I must speak a little further.

In 1881, when a young man of twenty-seven, Albert conceived and put into execution a brilliant and humane plan, which in this country, many years later, became well known as the "Big Brother" movement. He arranged with local authorities to be notified when a boy was discharged from the penitentiary, and Albert then took him in charge. He housed, fed and clothed him, taught him a trade, and showed him that one crime does not make a criminal, and that it was possible to save him, both for himself and for the community.

He arranged it in this way. In a set of rooms which his mother portioned off for him in her large apartment house, he opened a vocational school. He fitted up the place with the proper accommodations, so that his charges could live there, free of all expense, while they were getting their training. Then he engaged an instructor, and began a systematic campaign to help unfortunate or mistaken young boys to become useful both to themselves and to the world. So successful was he that it was not long before the authorities themselves took up his plan and carried it out on a larger scale than he could afford. Thus from his nucleus grew a chain of similar schools that reached into every corner of Russia.

He had a short, but glorious life—his name on the lips of all liberal Russians. He survived to see his efforts take effect, but no longer; for, after he had established several homes of this character in Odessa, consumption developed, and he died. There was not anyone, young or old, Jew or Christian, rich or poor, illiterate or enlightened, who did not follow him either in thought or in person to his last resting place. Every class was represented at his burial. As his fame spread so rapidly a multitude knew, loved and appreciated him.

I also wish to speak of Vladimir Chavkin. Years ago, while still in his early thirties, he was one of Pasteur's assistants. When the bubonic plague broke out in India he was one of the first to volunteer to risk his life for the furtherance of science and humanity. He undertook, as is now a matter of common knowledge, the inoculation of the sick. Fortunately his splendid efforts among the plague-stricken populace met with such success that his name became known all over the world.

The critical months of 1881 dragged by. The sky did not clear after the thunderclap. By the time autumn came a real movement toward emigration made itself evident in the thoughts and sentiments of the poorer Jews throughout their pale of settlement. The students who organized the "Self-Defense League" came together again to help shape and mold the Jewish sentiment and to bring the Jewish thought into practical channels. Accordingly they organized the "*Am-Ohlom*" (The Eternal People). This society was to decide upon a plan for emigration, and to help the needy with funds. Some favored Palestine; some the Argentine. My husband came out strongly in favor of the United States of America; and so the purpose of the *"Am-Ohlom"* was definitely settled as an aid and furtherance of emigration to America. Another of its objects was to show the world that a Jew was able to become a productive worker if given the proper chance. Thus agricultural colonization took shape in their imaginations as the chief objective for future time.

My husband was appointed one of the committee of the *"Am-Ohlom."* He opened a correspondence with the Jewish organizations in Cracow, Vienna, Paris and London, as well as with other Russian societies, for the purpose of raising funds. I do not know the exact amount of money collected, but I do know that responses were very generous, and many, many hundreds of the desperate people were helped to emigrate. (How my husband kept his health in those days I cannot tell. What with his regular college work, tutoring as a means of livelihood, and the work for the *"Am-Ohlom"* he rarely had more than five hours' sleep.)

In January 1882, the first party sent by the society, consisting of only six men—but those the very finest and most intelligent—left for Brody to wait and arrange there for the other parties to arrive. By May of 1882 three more parties left Odessa, this time hundreds going in each band. But when the government became aware of the large flow of emigration very stringent laws were promulgated, and it was impossible for the third party to obtain passports. To plan the work of the *"Am-Ohlom"* therefore became much more difficult, since an organization of this character was now prohibited by the government. Delegates from organizations in other towns were sent to us; the *"Am-Ohlom"* had to manipulate passports for all the emigrants to use, and yet keep its meetings secret.

Most of the conferences were held in the house of Nuchem Rubin. It so happened that on March 13 the head of the Odessa Gendarmerie, Strelnikoff, was assassinated. He had been sent from St. Petersburg to rout out the nest of revolutionists. He had filled the prisons to capacity with the best youth of Odessa. But, in spite of all his vigilance, he himself was struck down and the assassins escaped. The police were in a frenzy and more alert than ever. They noticed that an unusual number of people frequented the Rubin home. They became suspicious and, concluding that the meetings were of a political nature, hoped for a clue—for some connection with this last Terroristic act, the assassination of Strelnikoff. So they decided to raid the place in the course of a big meeting which was to be held March 16. One who took an active part in the *"Am-Ohlom"*—then a youth of eighteen, a delegate from Elizabetgrad—the late Dr. Hillel Solotaroff described the raid to me very dramatically:

> About sixty-nine members of the '*Am-Ohlom*' were present, and, during the heat of discussion, a late arrival ran in, pale and trembling.
>
> "We are surrounded by police and Cossacks!" he gasped.

No sooner had he uttered the words than the Captain of the Police, with several of his Cossacks, rushed in. Looking towards the very end of the room, where the speaker sat, the Captain said to his men:

"Take him! There he is!"

The man was brought forward, but the Captain looked at him and said:

"No, the description calls for a different person. The man we want is tall, slim, with big gray eyes, eye-glasses, a short beard. No, this fellow does not answer the description."

All present recognized that he was looking for my husband. By some lucky chance he was elsewhere and was not intending to report until the very end of the meeting. Fortunately, the police broke up the gathering. They took the names of those present, and ordered them to appear on the following day at the Police Station. My husband was advised early next morning by these friends, to leave the city and disappear for a week or so, until the trouble should blow over, as the Government suspected him of being a party to the assassination. He took the warning—the more willingly that by this time all work for the four parties about to emigrate was complete.

No more efforts could be made in this line for many reasons, the main one being the very strict police surveillance and their refusal to issue passports. By the end of May the last of the parties had left for America.

When my husband returned from his brief exile he went on with his studies and completed his third year at Law School.

On April 25th, 1882, we were married.

The first letters from the members of the "*Am-Ohlom*" in America—from men like the much-loved philosopher Bokal, from Dr. Paul Kaplan and from Dr. Solotaroff, came full of enthusiasm. Slowly but surely the decision was forming in my husband's mind to give up law, a profession in which he undoubtedly would have made a success, as he was considered by the faculty and the student body the most promising and brilliant man in the class. He had everything to gain by continuing with law, and had only one more year at the University. He had my father's promise of financial backing when he started to practice his profession, the ability to assist and ease life for his aged mother, to help his brothers, who had sacrificed so much to see him get his education-prospects most alluring. But sincerity in thought and purpose and great idealism were his outstanding characteristics. With his rigid uprightness and vivid sense of truth and justice, he felt that, as the leader of the "*Am-Ohlom*," it was not for him to choose a safe and free profession in Russia while others were, despite their enthusiastic letters, undoubtedly enduring hardships in America. Of all the student organizers of the Self-Defense League and later of the "*Am-Ohlom*" he was the only one to give up a sure career to take up the dark unknown; for, in June 1882, he decided to live up to the idea he was preaching—"Back to the

Land"—"Farming for the Jews in the New Land." He would actually be their teacher and leader, and, to equip himself, he would take up agriculture as a profession.

CHAPTER III
FROM LAW TO AGRICULTURE

There was a storm of reproach and disapproval from my parents when they heard of my husband's decision. Agriculture as a profession! To become a plain *mujik*—as they saw it. An occupation so far below the dignity of an intelligent, *balabatish* (respectable) Jewish youth! But his decision was irrevocable.

I was fully in sympathy with his idea and in July 1882, we left for Paris, which boasted a splendid agricultural college. There, upon investigation, we found that only single men could enter, as the college was located a few miles out of Paris and the students lived in dormitories.

However, we learned soon after that Zurich in Switzerland had an excellent agricultural college, and within a month we had left Paris and reached Zurich. Here we found quite a large and interesting colony of Russian students. My husband soon passed his entrance examinations and we settled down to a three-year stay.

It was during his third and last year that my husband wrote many articles on agriculture for the leading newspapers in Russia. These called forth splendid comment and the practical result was that a certain Maslinikoff of St. Petersburg, who in later years became Minister of Agriculture, asked him to write editorials on farming for an agricultural paper which he was soon to publish.

The course completed, in the summer of 1885 we returned to Odessa, as our friends in America, especially the late Dr. Paul Kaplan, begged us not to consider emigration at this time. All their dreams of colonization had been shattered. A few settlements formed in Oregon and Kansas were a total failure, and the colonists were all back in New York, working in various factories. So we decided on Odessa.

But even in so simple a venture as a journey back home my husband managed to achieve something. Two of our friends in Zurich, the well-known Pavel Axelrod and George Plechanov, were eager to smuggle into Russia a pamphlet which they had written, and which they had no way of sending and distributing, as the watch on the German frontier was sharp. Russia had made a secret treaty at this time, by which Germany was to arrest and deport any escaped Russian revolutionists, and to confiscate any radical literature that might be sent through her borders from England, France or Switzerland. By the action of this treaty, Leo Deutsch (a refugee well known here, in America, for the past twelve or thirteen years) was arrested on the German frontier when he left Zurich with a large supply of revolutionary literature, and handed over to the Russian authorities, who sentenced him to a long term of years in Siberia.

At this juncture Pavel Axelrod approached my husband. He told him that they had worked out a clever way of fooling the customs officials, if only he would be willing to undertake the serious mission. My husband readily consented.

This was the plan: We had a great many German and French scientific books. The bindings of these, consisting of sheets of paper subjected to heavy pressure and cloth-covered, were torn off. The revolutionary pamphlets were then pressed together, covered with binders' cloth, and the books re-bound. As the forbidden literature was printed on the very finest tissue paper, whole editions were thus smuggled into Russia.

When we arrived at Odessa the customs officials looked into our baggage and began to examine the trunks full of books. They could not read French or German, however, so they informed us that the boxes with our clothes could be sent forward, but that the trunks containing books would have to remain until they had been thoroughly searched. My husband would be notified, they said, when they had finished examining them.

The five following days were long and nerve-wracking, as may be imagined; but finally the notice from the Customs House came. Once more the authorities had been fooled by the shrewdness of the revolutionists! It had never entered their heads to rip open one of the bindings; and so my husband was spared the prisons and long years in Siberia that might have been his fate. As a matter of fact, most of the Russian customs officials, being ignorant men, were so stupid that the wide-awake revolutionists generally got the better of them. With a heart full of satisfaction and relief my husband shipped the books home at once, ripped off the bindings and mailed the pamphlets to their destinations, where they were further distributed throughout Russia and Siberia.

Close upon his return to Odessa, my husband, in quite high glee, accepted an offer from Maslinikoff as the assistant editor of the forthcoming agricultural paper. He waited impatiently for the assignment, but, instead, the newly-edited paper arrived with my husband's article printed in it, and a letter from Maslinikoff, saying that he was very sorry he would not be able to have him come to St. Petersburg, as the Swiss diploma deprived him of the right of settlement outside the pale.

The blow was hard. The question of a livelihood became again of pressing importance. The money received for articles already published had been spent as fast as it came. Not having a Russian diploma, my husband could not obtain a position as manager of an estate, for he was now compelled to live only within the pale. So he turned to his good old stand-by—tutoring.

CHAPTER IV
AMONG THE DON COSSACKS

In the early spring of 1888 my husband received a letter from a Professor Kusnetzoff, the director of a teachers' seminary in the Caucasus, in Eastern Russia, saying he had read my husband's articles in *Agriculture*; that he was very much interested in them and in the man who wrote them; that he had a big estate thirty versts from Yiesk; and that he would be very glad to secure my husband's services as manager of the estate.

Remembering his sad experience with Mr. Maslinikoff, editor of *Agriculture*, my husband answered Professor Kusnetzoff, asking him whether he realized that it was a Jew to whom he was offering the position. An answer came back stating that he "was above the question of race and creed." He "put character and manhood above all," he said, "and if willing to take the position, nobody need ever interfere with you in any way." He offered him six hundred rubles a year, with full maintenance for himself and family.

Always a man to whom money was distinctly a means and never an end in itself, my husband was well satisfied with the terms. Often have I heard him give expression to the freedom that he felt when his earnings were well disposed of—his monthly check sent to his mother; and later on to an older widowed sister, and his own modest requirements paid for. He would then say, gratefully, as one relieved of a burden: "No more money, no more worry! I have given it all where it belongs."

In accepting the offer from the Caucasus he was only too happy at the opportunity to do the work he had been preparing himself for in the previous three years.

In March 1886, my husband, our little daughter Marie and I left for Yiesk, a town east of Rostov, on the border of the Caucasus—the very heart of the country of the Don Cossacks. The estate consisted of about 2,000 acres of land. Parts of it were sub-leased to Letts, who had emigrated from Lapland several decades before, and the rest to the native Cossacks. My husband's mission was to bring the land that had been sub-leased to a higher degree of cultivation. The property was laid out mainly in small fruit orchards, yielding apples, pears, plums and grapes, and in large fields of rye, wheat and corn.

As soon as we arrived at the estate, a three-room house was built for us, and in this we bestowed ourselves comfortably and hopefully.

My husband's public-spiritedness, which played so great a part in his nature, showed itself immediately. First he called together all the tenants of the estate under his management and informed them that his knowledge was at their service; that he was always ready, nay, eager to give them advice in whatever capacity they needed it—agricultural advice above all. That whole summer, with one-half dozen men, he worked hard to improve the soil, the shrubs, the crops—not only to make them profitable, but to make of this big farm a model for his tenants and for all the farmers in the neighborhood, far and wide. He was the broadly enlightened agriculturist who knew of the latest and best ways of tilling the soil, among a very ignorant and backward peasantry. From near and far they began to come to him for advice. The very first year showed good results from his improved methods. The peasants took eager note of it and his name was on everyone's lips.

The hard summer and fall season over, my husband started a course of lectures on "The Right Way of Tilling the Soil." Peasants would come, rain or shine, with their wives and grown-up sons and daughters, often from versts and versts around. The big empty barn saw life. It was crowded to its full capacity with peasants, very eager to learn and to devour every word. And after the lectures were over, the farmers would talk about many a topic of the day, hurling question after question at my husband, so that time and again it would be well after midnight before the gatherings broke up. These gatherings took place Saturday evenings, and eagerly did the neighbors wait for those Saturdays to come! What a source of enlightenment it was for them! If any of the tenants and neighbors knew, or even surmised, that the man they grew to be so fond of, the man they looked up to as a true friend, the man they could go to in any kind of trouble, and who always not only lent them a sympathetic ear, but stretched out the hand of friendship and helped remove whatever obstacle was in their way, if, I say, these men surmised that the manager was a Jew, they never in any way made us feel it. They all felt too great an admiration for the Christlike kindliness of the man; and this they soon had additional cause to value.

That very winter diphtheria broke out among the children in one of the villages about three miles from our estate, and in a few days nearly all the children were victims of the terrible pestilence. The ignorance of the peasants was unbounded. The only doctor they had was a quack, who lived many miles away. As soon as my husband heard of the trouble, he drove to the stricken village. He found no quarantine whatever. The sick and the well, young and old, slept in one large bed in the one room, where also were herded for protection from the bitter cold the new-born calf and lamb, the ducks and chickens, all huddled together as was quite customary. And the windows were kept tightly shut! The stifling air and the condition of the room may be imagined!

The first thing my husband did was to drive over to Yiesk, the nearest town, which was very fortunate in having a physician it could call its own. This man was a true friend of the peasant and the poor laboring man. He was the leading spirit of every progressive undertaking in that town and had become a devoted friend of my husband's, who knew that he would find a responsive chord in the doctor's heart. He had no trouble in bringing him back at once, with all the necessary medicines. They separated the dangerously sick from those who could be saved, and together they did whatever could be done to prevent the spread of the malady. Of the twenty-two children in this village, only seven survived.

A week later my husband started a course of lectures on "Health and Sanitation," the doctor friend helping him with material for the lectures. A collection was taken up from all the families in the neighboring villages, and a supply of necessary drugs was purchased and installed in each.

Exceedingly interesting were these two years we spent far away from civilization, but in close touch with people for whom we could do so much. There was work for me to do, as well as my husband, for while he was away lecturing and talking to the older folk, I taught the youngsters reading and arithmetic. There was no school anywhere within miles.

A few glimpses of the standards and character of the people among whom we lived may be in place here. They were a mixture of Letts and of Don Cossacks, freely intermarried. Often, on Sunday afternoon, my husband and I would sit on the steps of our bungalow, and several neighbors, with their families, young and old, would join us. I remember one Sunday afternoon, we were sitting and talking on various topics of interest to the peasants, and my husband asked one of them the reason why nearly every peasant—even those who were quite young—have a second and sometimes a third wife. The answer came: "Child-birth and the complications that often followed." These were, in nearly every case, the cause of death. And no wonder! Whenever a woman gave birth to a child, especially if it happened during the summer months—during harvest, when every hand was needed in the field—as soon as she had received first aid from an elderly woman neighbor or some quack, a doctor was miles away and time too precious for anyone to drive for him—she was not only left alone, but expected to take full charge of all the burdens of the most primitive peasant household. And it should be remembered that during the harvest there are two or three extra men hired to help gather in the crops, and that these are additional mouths for her to feed. Naturally at times the strain would be too great and she would die. Several times I was astonished to find a woman who had given birth to a child a day or two previously at the family wash tub, or cooking the dinner, or kneading the family supply of coarse black bread, a task which alone would tax the strength of any man. So much for the legend about the easy childbirth of the peasant woman!

Once a young peasant, married only two years, and known as quite a model husband, stepped in, and during our conversation asked me: "How often does your husband beat you?"

I caught my breath at the question, but looking into his face saw that he inquired in dead earnest, and to tell him that my husband never gave me a beating would appear to him a very poor joke indeed. So I answered: "About once a year. Sometimes twice—before the biggest holidays."

He nodded approvingly. "You see, Barina" (Lady), he remarked, "I give my wife a beating on or before every holiday. (And in Russia they do come very, very often.) "You know," he continued, "the best of wives will never respect or think much of her man unless he gives her a sound beating now and then."

Among the Russian proverbs is one, and a proverb usually tells the tale: "Love your wife as your own soul, but shake her like a pear tree."

I remember, however, the case of a woman who my husband saved from a different sort of beating. The story will also serve to show the respect in which the peasants held him. We had one farmer, a Cossack, who was married to a Lettish woman. He and his family shared one isbah (cabin) with his father-in-law, a common arrangement among the peasants. The old man kept his savings of a lifetime, about one thousand rubles, in his trunk. Few of the peasants were enlightened enough to keep their money in a bank; and the bank, in most cases, was miles away. One day the old man found out that the money—all his savings—was gone. His suspicions at once fell on his son-in-law, who was a drunkard, and who beat his wife not only on or before a holiday but whenever the spirit moved him—and that was oftener that I should like to tell. His father-in-law and his wife reproached him, and in a drunken rage he picked up an axe and ran after his wife. Their cabin was about a block from our bungalow. She ran straight for our house, screaming: "Save me! Save me! Petrich is at my heels to kill me!"

My husband, who was standing outside the house and saw from afar the drunkard running, pushed the terrified woman inside our door and closed it on her. He himself stood there defenseless to meet the frenzied man. Seeing my husband so cool before him, he seemed to sober in a moment, and then my husband, in a tense, commanding voice, exclaimed: "Stop, Petrich! Have you lost your mind to run wild with an axe? Give it to me at once!"

The instinctive awe and respect that any peasant has for authority won the day. As by a miracle, without a word, he handed the axe to my husband, and the woman's life was saved.

Another incident will show the sentiment of the peasants towards my husband. The nephew whom my grandmother brought with her on a visit, and left with us during the winter, was an exceedingly mischievous lad of twelve. One day, while playing in a peasant's isbah, he approached the ikon, and cut off the legs and pierced the eyes of a picture of St. Nicholas that hung on the wall. This was a crime against religion unpardonable, especially when committed by a Jewish boy. In any other part of Russia such an act would have immediately led to a Pogrom. As it was the peasant swore vengeance. He was a very bitter and quarrelsome man, so we had reason to be anxious. Unhappily, too, a few days later, his little daughter, a child of six, became sick and died. Before she fell ill, she had had a childish quarrel with our nephew, and he had given her a spanking. And now she was dead. The peasant had, seemingly, sufficient reason for a deep grudge against us.

While the funeral was in full progress and my husband entered the house to offer our condolences, the father of the girl stood up, and amid a dead silence exclaimed, pointing at my husband: "His nephew, the Jew, killed my child!"

The situation was critical, but one of the oldest and most respected men among them rose and said: "Michailich, have you a heart? Have you no fear of God? This is not the time to wrangle. Besides, we all know Gregory Konstantinovich too well and know what he has done and is doing for all of us to lay blame to him. What troubles are you brewing? If his nephew did wrong, we will see to it later. Let us proceed, and do not let us defame the holy services of the funeral further."

By the nodding of the heads of all present one could see that they were in full accord with the sentiments expressed by their elder. Thus a situation that might have ended tragically was relieved.

I recall also another Sunday afternoon. The sun is sinking low, shedding its last glorious rays on the large orchard before us, and gilding as far as the eye can reach the full ripe ears of corn, rye and wheat. From afar the bleating of the flock is heard, the shepherds bringing it in. Soon the white masses of the sheep are seen huddled against the sky. Nearer and nearer they come—the whole large field covered thickly, as with a snowy weed. The flaming tops of the golden grain furnish a rich foreground. Among the dim masses we can soon distinguish the figures of the shepherds and hear their songs and cries mingled with the bleating of the flock. Closer and closer comes the weird music of the balalaikas—the rich sound of the concertina. The songs, the instruments, the whistling, the bleating of the sheep all produce a confused but intense harmony. The setting sun, the thousands of shifting, surging bodies, the sun-kissed grain seem to make up a huge stage-setting, depicting the pastoral life of these simple peasants. That scene has left an impression on me which lasts to this day.

To add to the brilliance of the picture, both the men and the women had their best Sunday clothes on. The women wore their gay colored, four-yard-wide short skirts, with the blouses of snowy-white homespun linen, low-necked, wide-sleeved, richly embroidered in blue and red cross-stitch work. Each had a wide, bright sash about her waist, and on her bosom beads of every color, every description, row on row. To complete the richness and gaiety of that national costume there were ribbons—some of them fastening the long braids of hair that hung down the back, and some going to tie up the beads. Never was there a more brilliant and tantalizing display of color. The men in their Sunday attire were a fine sight too—short breeches of cloth or velvet tucked into the high boots; over the breeches a gay red shirt, buttoned on one side (called, for that reason, *koso-vorotko*); a bright girdle giving additional dash of color; and, to complete the costume, a high cap which only the Don Cossacks wear in Russia, and which only they know how to wear!

The ensemble was so enchanting that, inspired by it, my husband asked a girl and boy of about seventeen, who were known as good dancers, to dance for us. Everybody was glad to do what would please Gregory Konstantinovich. So, some of the shepherds passing by with their instruments were called, and then we saw the real Russian dance. The girl and boy were beautiful types of the Don Cossack—pure, unmixed blood was theirs. Tall, graceful, with the athletic vigor that only ever-outdoor life can give, their faces strong and handsome with the traits that centuries of warrior forefathers had impressed upon them, in richly colored national costume, they presented an unforgettable picture. Nearby, in front of the big barn, was a platform. We settled ourselves around it. Then, to the music of concertinas, mouth organs and balalaikas, accompanied by whistling and singing and clapping of hands from the whole crowd, they started. I have seen many a dancer in later years, but the pagan grace and joy of life expressed in every movement—the dash, the fire, the wonderful setting Nature provided, has never, to my mind, been excelled or equaled.

But the pleasant memories of our life among the peasants draw to a close.

Ten miles away, in a neighboring *stanitza*, as the Cossack villages are called, lived the old father of the man who owned the estate. He was an orthodox priest. He had been taught that the Jews had killed Jesus Christ; that the Jews were a far inferior race; that the Jews kill innocent Christian children and use their blood to make Passover matzos; that all Jews were usurers; and such other ugly distortions of fact as the Russian Government

49

could use to fling among the dark, ignorant masses of people, to avert their attention from the real causes of trouble.

To this old priest every Jew was a most hateful person. Besides, long before he found out that my husband was a Jew, he developed a grudge against him. It was the old man's custom to come to the estate and carry away loads of fruit, vegetables, corn and whatever he could lay his hands on. He expected to do the same thing while my husband was the manager on his son's estate. Now, while my husband was perfectly willing to let him have a reasonable quantity of the produce for his home table, he would not allow an extravagant robbing of the farms, as he had to show the owner the practical results of his farming methods. A clash could hardly be avoided.

It happened that my husband's grandmother decided to come and visit us, and she set out without informing us beforehand. She stopped at the *stanitza*, at the priest's house, to inquire how to reach her grandson. Then only did he find out that the man who was managing his son's estate was a Jew. This was more than his pious Christian soul could bear. He began to bombard his son with letters, imploring him to consider what he was doing, begging him to think of his soul—his afterlife. And although his son had written to my husband again and again to tell him how much he was pleased with the improvements and the results obtained in so short a time from his methods; how much he appreciated the splendid relation between my husband, the tenants and all the neighboring villagers, yet the passionate, incessant appeals of the father to his son had their effect.

In February 1887, with our two daughters, Marie and Vera, we left for America. The two experiences, one with the editor of *Agriculture*, and the other with the owner of the Caucasus estate, showed my husband clearly that with his profession he could have no place in Russia. In June 1887, on the steamer "Fulda," with two thousand rubles given us by my mother, we arrived in New York. Dr. Kaplan and a few other friends met us at Castle Garden.

CHAPTER V
FACING THE NEW WORLD

Can you imagine all the hopes and dreams that were fluttering in our hearts on our arrival?

Yet the first encouraging words of our friend Kaplan were: "For God's sake, why did you come here? I sent two letters imploring you to remain at home!"

We had left, however, before his letters reached us. Not that it would have made any difference if we had received them. We had no choice but to emigrate.

A cousin of mine, a photographer named Solomon Kaufman, was among those who waited for us on arrival. He took us to his home on Eldridge Street, where he, his wife, their baby and a boarder were living in a two-room flat.

I must mention here a singular incident in which a fellow passenger of ours played a chief part. With us on the steamer was a Pole who my husband had befriended on the trip. As he had not a soul to go to, my cousin very kindly offered him hospitality for a few days, until he should find himself. On the following day the young Pole left the house, saying that he was going out for a stroll. That was the very last we ever saw or heard of him. His valise and his few belongings were never claimed. He must have been lost trying to find his way home. The confusing sameness of the streets and houses must have misled him, and owing to his inability to speak either English or Jewish, he was swallowed up in the mammoth city. All our search for him was fruitless. Whoever has read that wonderful story of Korolenko's "After Bread," will remember that the plot deals with a very similar incident, except that there the central figure is a girl.

We stayed for several days at my cousin's, who did his utmost to make us comfortable. The first evening the little flat was breathlessly hot. When bedtime came, my cousin, draping himself in a sheet and taking a pillow in his hand, casually remarked that he and his boarder were going up to the roof to sleep, and if we wished, we could follow him, as it really was airier there! It looked so novel—so funny to me, that we decided to follow his example. And when, wrapped in sheets, our pillows in hand, we reached the roof, we saw, as far as the eye could reach, white figures stretched out on all the adjoining roofs. Certainly it would have been stifling to sleep indoors, so, after another laugh, I settled down to the good night's rest which our fatigue insured us.

A few nights later, when we went to sleep at another friend's place, Krimonts, the same funny thing happened. Towards midnight, young and old, wrapped in white sheets, made a procession toward the roof. These friends of mine had another trouble. They did not know how to get rid of the bedbugs which were thick in the walls. They were of exceedingly careful habits, and kept their rooms scrupulously clean, but it seemed that only the burning of the tenement they lived in would have saved them from the pest.

We had been just a week in America when an older brother of my husband's, whom he had helped to escape from military service in Russia and had sent off to America with the second party of the "*Am-Ohlom,*" heard of our arrival in New York. He was living in Pittsfield, Massachusetts, where he had a small picture frame store. He came to see us and advised my husband to take his family and go with him to Pittsfield, "*sich ausgerünen,*" as he remarked. The following day we left for Pittsfield. My husband became the utility man in his brother's picture store.

The rapidity with which he learned English is worthy of mention. His brother and his brother's friends, who were nearly all illiterate men, were amazed that a man only a week in this country should read the English-printed papers and understand the gist of them as well as they, who were five years in the country. It seemed miraculous to them. But a man who had had six or seven years of Latin, Greek, German and French would naturally read English and understand it without much effort. For two weeks my husband helped to make picture frames, and made himself generally useful about the store. But his education, particularly his knowledge of chemistry, made him feel he could use his abilities to better advantage. His brother suggested peddling matches, saying that, to his knowledge, every successful man in America had started just that way.

If peddling was the first step necessary to success, my husband was willing to try it; only he thought he would apply his knowledge to it. He bought all necessary chemicals from a traveling peddler and bottles of all kinds and sizes, many of them far from dainty and beautiful. What was his idea? On our big kitchen stove he began to make perfumes! Several unexpected explosions occurred, one of which set the chimney afire. In the chimney, as it happened, we kept our official papers and documents. They were all burned.

In about three weeks, after all kinds of difficulties, after various experiments and failures, during which both he and the house were in lively danger of being burned, he had a stock of perfumes ready to sell. To peddle his own manufactured goods was much more dignified than to sell matches, my husband felt.

Pittsfield had many factory villages on its outskirts. With a newly purchased satchel, heavily laden with his bottles, he set out to dispose of his perfumes. In his fine European suit of clothes, with his intelligent face and refined, gentle, sympathetic manner, he made a striking appearance. The people were used to seeing pack peddlers, but never a peddler who looked like that before! From factory to factory, from village to village he walked. Hardly ever did anybody refuse to buy, and he would come home exhausted, with an empty valise. Still, after two months of very hard work he found that he could not provide suitably for himself and his family.

Meanwhile our friends had written us advising us to return to New York City. They had heard of the wonderful success my husband was making in manufacturing and selling perfumes. The five months of our stay in Pittsfield had, indeed, been beneficial in one way. We lived there among Americans only, and *nolens volens* we had to speak English; so that, in the five months we learned to converse in that language. Back to New York now my husband went in search of work. After fruitless wandering for two weeks, he was told by a friend, studying at Columbia University—that same Dr. Kaplan—that one Henry Rice was looking for a chemistry tutor for his son. My husband went to see Mr. Rice, whose son was to be prepared for the Columbia entrance examination. Everything was comfortably settled, when the question of a laboratory came up. Fortunately Dr. Kaplan knew a professor, Baron de Taube, a Russian by birth, who kept a private preparatory school for boys. My husband went to see him, and Baron de Taube was more than pleased to allow the use of his laboratory. So the very next day the agreement with Mr. Rice to prepare his son for college, teaching him daily from ten to twelve, was made, for the princely sum of ten dollars a week.

It seemed wealth to us then. The two thousand rubles that we had brought with us when we came to America were gone. Before the pupil in chemistry appeared, the world had looked quite dark for us. We were at rock bottom. Dr. Solotaroff, who had been one of the members of the "Defense League" and of the "*Am-Ohlom*," and who was very fond of my husband, found out at that time that we were in New York. (He had been living with his parents in Cincinnati when we first arrived.) As soon as he could discover our address, he came to see us, unfortunately at a time when there was neither bread nor sugar nor tea nor kerosene in the house. We had no food of any kind left, and we were thinking of pawning some of our jewelry. Although as students in Zurich we had very often pawned our jewelry and silver to help needy friends, this was the first time we had faced doing so for ourselves. Dr. Solotaroff had last seen us at our wedding, in my father's beautiful home in Odessa, where everything spoke not only of comfort, but of luxury. He was of an exceedingly emotional nature. He burst into tears, but, finally controlling himself, he left the house. He soon returned with bread and sugar and tea and cuts of cold meat. We had a feast indeed. This timely help was enough to bridge over the bad days. Within a week my husband began to teach and the wolf was kept from the door.

Meanwhile Dr. Solotaroff wrote a letter to a friend of his, Professor Warden, of Washington, D. C., Vice President of the American Chemical Society, about Mr. Sabsovich and his qualifications as an agricultural chemist. Dr. Warden replied, saying that my husband was just the sort of man who could readily be employed in one of the thirty-nine agricultural experiment stations being opened with, but independent of, the State agricultural colleges. He enclosed the names and addresses of all the directors who were to be in charge of these stations. Our friend came to us after college hours—he was a medical student at the time—and wrote letters for us to the various directors, until all had been applied to. A few days later answers began to pour in. Some few laboratories were already opened; others were just about to be opened; some were being built; others had not yet been started. However, the correspondence soon narrowed down to five directors of existing laboratories.

In connection with these applications a funny incident took place. While being interviewed by the director of the Geneva (N. Y.) Experiment Station, whom he met at the Astor House, my husband was asked "What are your ambitions?"

He answered: "Why, I have no ambitions."

Undoubtedly the head of the Geneva Laboratory must have been puzzled by this reply. My husband took the word "ambition" in the sense that the Russian intelligentzia understood it, namely, as greed for conquest, getting ahead at any price, at any cost. When next he met Dr. Solotaroff and Dr. Kaplan and told them of the strange question and the answer he had given, they roared with laughter. They had been in the country for five years, and knew in just what sense the word "ambition" is interpreted by an American.

We had a wide circle of friends in New York, who met each other frequently for one purpose or another. Occasionally a dance was given for some cause we were interested in, and lectures delivered on various subjects. When the night of our first dance arrived my husband insisted that I go to it with our friends; he wouldn't have me miss that pleasure, but would stay at home with the children; saying that he would go to the lectures, and that would be a fair division. But when a very interesting lecture came up, he would surprise me by having some friend stay with the children, explaining: "Not for the world would I go alone and have you miss this pleasure!"

He was a home body primarily and liked best, after the day's work was over, to stay there, seated in a comfortable chair, with a book as his companion. He liked now and then to visit a friend, or to go to the theatre, or to a dance given by the community. But to have a few intimates in his own home, and to discuss matters with them until the small hours of the morning, was his chief delight.

I well remember that spring of 1887. We lived in 86th Street, near the East River. The boys—Dr. Solotaroff, Dr. Kaplan, the late Nickolai Aleinikoff and others—would come for a weekend to the country—86th Street!—to visit us. At one or two a.m. I would leave them still discussing some book, some philosophic theory, or interesting question of the day.

In May young Mr. Rice successfully passed his chemistry examinations for Columbia, and the lessons ceased. Fortunately, within a very few days a letter came from Dr. O'Brien, director of the Fort Collins Agricultural Experiment Station, with whom my husband had been in correspondence for several months. He was asked whether he could come to Fort Collins in a week's time, and, if so, to wire his conditions. Dr. O'Brien was going to be married and wanted an assistant at once. Then the question arose: How and where was my husband to get the money for the journey to Colorado, not to mention what must be left for his family until the first check could be drawn? My husband had met Mr. Rice several times, and felt that he could go and talk to him. So he showed him Dr. O'Brien's letter.

"You certainly are not going to turn down such an offer, are you?" said Mr. Rice.

"Certainly not, if I can borrow the money to get there, and leave some for my family here," answered my husband.

"Oh, that's all right! Just name the sum, and don't worry about the rest," assured our new friend, handing my husband $250.

On his way home my husband wired Dr. O'Brien: "$1,000 a year. Will arrive at Fort Collins within a week."

CHAPTER VI
PIONEERING WITH PIONEERS

When Mr. Sabsovich reached Fort Collins Dr. O'Brien left on a three weeks' honeymoon.

My husband was in full charge of the laboratory. Having been but one year in the country he had not yet a perfect command of the language, and was not quite sure whether his interpretations would be always exact. He had engaged in chemical analysis only while he was a student and not since that time. Thus, being of a very shy nature, it suited him admirably to be left entirely alone at the very beginning of the work. During those three weeks he worked for Dr. O'Brien fifteen hours daily, Sundays included, until he found he had a full grasp of the work. When his chief returned he could not compliment his new assistant sufficiently on the splendid results obtained in the analyses of soils, foods, and so on; apart from the look of the laboratory in general. The biggest thing was now accomplished. My husband felt at ease, for he knew then that he could handle the work.

Six weeks later my two daughters, Marie and Vera, and I joined him in Colorado. We found a nice little home, one or two blocks away from the College, and furnished it on the instalment plan with monthly payments of six dollars. Twelve dollars went back each month, to pay off the $250 so kindly lent to us, and about eight dollars regularly to my husband's mother. We still had about $35 a month left for our table. We had plenty of wearing apparel, brought with us from Russia, and, considering the cost of living in a small Western town, or rather village, over thirty years ago, we managed to get along quite comfortably.

Life was very pleasant, and, on the whole, interesting in this small college town. We were made welcome in the college colony, and soon felt at home with our neighbors. That winter my husband suggested to some members of the staff the organization of a club, to be called: "You and I," where once a week the members (everybody eligible) would come together and discuss topics of the day, sometimes having a little music or a sociable. The suggestion was taken up, the club organized, and we spent many a pleasant evening that way.

On March 18th our third daughter, Nellie, was born, and in May, very dear friends of ours, Mr. and Mrs. Moses Livshis, who had settled as farmers in Kansas, about 180 miles from Topeka, wrote to us, saying they had a large farm on which they were raising cattle. They told us how wonderful their prospects were, and that if my husband wanted to save a little money, it would be a good idea to send his family to the farm. The living would cost next to nothing, as we would have to pay only for the groceries. Anything that the farm raised would not count at all, and whatever money my husband could save would be used to buy cattle and give him an interest in the ranch.

The farmer's wife and I had been girlhood chums. For my husband, therefore, the attraction was not the saving part, but my joy in visiting a friend whom I had not seen for many years. We tried that plan during the summer, but late in the fall the children and I returned to Fort Collins, as my husband couldn't stand the separation from his family any longer.

I must mention here one instance of his humanity and broad tolerance. One day, at noon, he, passing the school grounds, noticed that all the children were out playing in the yard, except a little colored girl of about five years, or even younger (just a kindergarten tot), who stood alone, seemingly unhappy and forlorn. That evening at supper time my husband asked his eldest daughter, Marie, who was in the kindergarten too, why the little colored girl was left alone and why nobody played with her. Was it that she was a bad child?

"No," answered Marie. "Just nobody plays with her because she is black."

"Don't you think it wrong to do a thing like that to a little girl for no fault of hers?" asked my husband.

"Would you object to playing with her? Fancy if you should be left alone just because you are the only little Jewish girl in your school? (As was the case.) Would you like it?"

Marie considered a moment, and then shook her head. "Sure, I'm going to play with her!" she said.

During the second year of my husband's stay at Fort Collins, articles on Russia, written by someone who signed herself "Princess X" began to appear in one of the leading Denver daily papers. The purpose of the articles was to influence the American people in favor of the Russian autocracy. "The Czar is as kind to his people—the peasants especially, as a loving father to his children!" My husband read these articles. Knowing that the homes of the peasants were often transformed into hells as a result of the Czar's fatherly ruling, he felt intensely indignant at these lies, and at once wrote an answer to them, which was published.

A few days later he received a letter from Miss Scott-Sexton, a well-known woman in Denver, and a person of high intelligence and culture. She told my husband in her letter how much she had enjoyed his protests, and said that she would like to meet him. She felt that the articles of "Princess X" must have been subsidized by the Russian Government. We extended her an invitation to come and spend a weekend at Fort Collins. The following Saturday she came to see us. She was eager to hear all about Russia, its government, its church, the peasants, the intelligentzia, the relations existing between one body and another. For two days my husband was talking, talking, talking. She was so much impressed by all she heard from a man whom one could not for a moment doubt to be all sincerity and uprightness, that she asked him to give several talks on Russia in the neighboring churches.

"The people here," she said, "are so utterly ignorant about the state of affairs in Russia, they are fed on such deliberate falsehood as those articles of the 'Princess X,' that enlightened, sincere and trustworthy information like yours would be much appreciated."

Glad of an opportunity to spread the truth about Russia, my husband accepted the invitation. For four or five consecutive Sundays he spoke on that topic in the churches of the neighborhood, with introductory remarks by Miss Scott-Sexton.

Meanwhile his responsibilities in the laboratory grew. In December 1888, a well-known lawyer of Fort Collins was found dead, and his wife was accused of poisoning him. The trial was held in Denver and Dr. O'Brien was chosen as the chemical expert to give the court and jury an analysis of the contents of the murdered man's stomach. The case was an exceedingly complicated one, and it kept Dr. O'Brien in Denver for three months, on and off. Not only the laboratory but the classroom had to be left under my husband's care. Since he was a boy of eleven, tutoring and teaching had been second nature to him. Time and time again the students would come to him, telling him how much they enjoyed his classes, how clear and simple he made the work. Frequently, too, the director of the college complimented him upon the work he was doing in the laboratory and the classroom, dwelling especially on the fact that the students seemed to be so fond of him. A group of students would often drop in and spend an hour or so at the house.

CHAPTER VII
A CALL TO THE LAND

In January 1889, my husband received letters from old friends in New York saying that large funds had been donated to America by Baron de Hirsch, of France, the money to be used in settling Jewish immigrants on the land as farmers. Dr. Kaplan, Herman Rosenthal and Selig Rosenbluth had been asked by the Committee appointed to administer the Fund, to join them and help them with their great task. They were representative of the intelligent Russians of the East Side. The members of the American Committee of the Baron de Hirsh Fund were among the best known persons in New York. Such men as Jacob Schiff, Dr. Julius Goldman, Judge M. S. Isaacs, the late James H. Hoffman, Oscar Straus, Henry Rice, William B. Hackenburg and Judge Mayer Sulzberger, of Philadelphia, served on the Committee.

A month later another letter came asking my husband to give in writing his ideas upon the subject of "Farming for the Russian Jew." With great enthusiasm indeed he took up this task. The old dream that like a flame smoldered in his heart blazed up, and that never-forgotten "Back to the Land" cry awoke in him again.

The Russian Jew, who of necessity has become solely a trader, might yet, he thought, as a farmer, rejuvenate his race. Many times that winter he told me how much joy it had given him to write those letters on "The Jew and Farming" for the Baron de Hirsch Fund. How much he dreamed of the realization of his hopes for the Jews as farmers!

One Tuesday in May 1890, my husband received a telegram asking him to take eight days' leave, if possible, in order to be in New York on the following Sunday afternoon, to be present at a committee meeting of the Baron de Hirsch Fund. He did not have the shadow of an idea that to attend this meeting would mean a change in all his future life and that of his family; that he would be leaving a quiet, peaceful life—the life of a scientist, of a college professor—for one of turbulence, excitement, misunderstanding, worries, and nerve-wracking anxieties; that he would have to deal with classes of people so widely different from one another—the Jewish immigrant, quite uncouth and raw in some cases, and the executive members of the Board of Directors, the highly cultured product of the best American standards, poor workingmen, rich employers of immigrant labor, foreign school boys and American instructors in the agricultural school later founded by my husband. Their ways of thinking, their sentiments, differed so widely that to make them understand each other and to sense each other's point of view would have been a staggering task for even an older and more experienced man.

With no thoughts like these in mind he went to the president of the college and showed him the telegram. Dr. O'Brien very kindly consented to the eight days' leave. With his daughter Marie, who could hardly ever be parted from her father, he left for New York. Exactly what took place at the meeting of the Baron de Hirsch Fund Committee, that following Sunday, I do not know; but on Monday I received a telegram, saying:

> Get ready. Am coming to take you and children to New York.

To say that I was surprised is saying very little. Neither my husband nor I had had the slightest inkling of an offer to manage the proposed Jewish Colony awaiting him at that Sunday conference. He told me how surprised and pleased he had been when upon entering the room, a man came forward and greeted him with outstretched hands. That man was the only one present whom he knew, being none other than Henry Rice, who had helped him to get to Fort Collins. My husband felt the pleasure of meeting him the more keenly, as by this time he had paid off the debt.

When my husband returned and told the president of the college that he had come back to resign, the president was dumfounded.

"Professor Sabsovich," he said, "you know that at our last meeting we voted an increase in your salary and the Board will decide on another very soon, because we would hate to lose you. All of us, both the faculty and students, appreciate the value of your services."

Though my husband knew that the sentiments of everyone in the college were of the warmest, still he was surprised and deeply touched by the president's words. He told him that no money consideration had played a part in the change he was making; he was to take up work for a cause that had been the dream of many years, for which, several years previously, he had sacrificed his home and his prospects in the legal profession, far better paying than any professorship and certainly more than the social work he was to undertake now. He made it clear that only work for the good of his own people, work that he had dreamed of for years, led him to resign. As a matter of fact, when the Baron de Hirsch Fund Committee, upon engaging him, asked what salary he would consider proper, he answered promptly: "My present salary." And this was $1,200 a year.

Three days later we left for New York. While in the Fort Collins station a telegram was handed to my husband which read:

We offer you the chair of Agricultural Chemistry.
Answer.   PRESIDENT,
                                Wyoming College.

Needless to say he replied: "Regret, but it is impossible."

On arriving in New York my husband found the administrative organization completed and work awaiting him. The board to administer the Baron de Hirsch

Fund was made up as follows: Judge M. S. Isaacs, Jacob H. Schiff, Jesse Seligman, Dr. Julius Goldman, Henry Rice, Judge Mayer Sulzberger, Honorable Oscar Straus, William B. Hackenburg and James H. Hoffman.

Let me say here that these men of high purpose and ideals and their successors were ever an inspiration to my husband and he enjoyed the full confidence of the trustees throughout his twenty-five years of affiliation with the Fund. To carry their plans into effective execution was always a source of keenest pleasure to him.

With the presidents of the Fund, who have been three since its inception: Judge Isaacs, Dr. Julius Goldman and the present incumbent, Eugene S. Benjamin, he was always in close contact. Of the original Board only Judge Sulzberger remains in office. The additional new members are: Mortimer L. Schiff, Herbert H. Lehman, Max J. Kohler, Judge Nathan Bijur, S. G. Rosenbaum, Abram I. Elkus, Charles L. Bernheimer, Alfred Jaretzki, S. F. Rothschild, S. S. Fleisher and Julius Rosenwald.

CHAPTER VIII
OPENING OF THE WOODBINE TRACT

Several parcels of land for the new colony had at once been offered and my husband's first duty, as superintendent of the enterprise, was to select the right one. With Herman Rosenthal, who was to be in charge of the New York office where applicants were received, Selig Rosenbluth and Dr. Kaplan, he visited several, among them the 3,000 acres in southern New Jersey, that is the Woodbine Colony of today.

It was cheap land, but, apart from that consideration, the Committee had other reasons for making the choice. For purposes of raising fruit, vegetables and corn it was very good. My husband told me that although there were undoubtedly better localities insofar as marketing facilities went, and richer soils, the Committee would rather spend the difference in preparing the land for the future farmer, enriching it according to modern scientific methods. The Woodbine Tract was bought August 11, 1891.

My husband, with twelve picked "pioneer farmers," left for Woodbine. None of the men had much money and hardly one of them could speak English or knew anything about farming. What is today a thrifty town surrounded by farms, consisted then of just a railroad station, one house owned by an old couple, and a shanty across the track. All this was so thickly surrounded by woods as far as the eye could reach that I remember we always feared the children might stray away and become lost therein. A single track of the West Jersey Railroad passed through, and the main occupation of those who lived nearby was woodchopping, although there was also an occasional farmer.

Of the six-roomed houses quickly erected, my husband chose one for his home. He then bought thirteen big straw hats and thirteen pairs of overalls, and with his twelve pioneer farmers began to measure off the woods. In this undertaking he had the expert help of the surveyor from Dennisville, the nearest village. Those were real pioneer times! With just a blanket and pillow under each one, all thirteen slept right on the floor. Certainly nobody could accuse my husband of being an aristocrat or behaving like one!

He was scrupulously careful of every cent he was obliged to spend of the Fund's money. He always felt that money spent carelessly might deprive another immigrant of the chance of becoming a farmer. While traveling about, looking for land, he and his three associates economized even on their food. Instead of taking their meals at a hotel, they would buy a few sandwiches and milk from a neighboring farmer.

In a few months new applicants began to arrive. By November and December 1891, there were sixty, all

Woodbine As We Found It

picked men. A widow, with several children and cousin of one of our farmers, was given the use of the other six-room house just opposite the one my husband selected for a home. She was to provide food for all those who were willing to board with her. A big barn was erected for the sixty men to live in temporarily and a great stove installed. Those sitting close to it felt warm, while the rest had to use their imaginations a good deal. So much for the accommodations.

A practical farmer, Frederick Schmidt, was engaged as assistant to my husband. He had very hard work at the start, surveying and dividing the land into farms. Each of the farmers was allotted thirty acres of land, which he was to clear for himself. In order to avoid a suggestion of pauperizing the settler, the Fund paid him for preparing his soil for cultivation, inasmuch as there was no other method of gaining a livelihood. Later on, in paying for the farm, sums advanced when the land was in process of preparation for cultivation were added to the cost of the farm.

As the Jews were totally inexperienced in this work of chopping down trees and pulling up tree-stumps, the labor seemed to them as difficult as tearing down the Egyptian pyramids. We must not forget that, as a rule, these men had never done any hard, physical labor before. They were mostly tradesmen. To encourage them, to show them that the work was not terribly hard in itself, only seeming so on account of their inexperience, several woodchoppers from Dennisville were employed to work alongside of them. The inexperienced beginner and the professional chopper were paid alike, just as an encouragement to the immigrant farmer; for, if he had not been paid for his labor, he would have thrown up his hands in disgust too early in the venture. Needless to say, the productiveness of the old-time woodchopper was incomparably higher than that of the future farmer; but paying them alike for widely different results served a certain big purpose. The future farmer was being slowly but surely acclimated. He was getting used to hard physical labor and making a living wage at the same time.

Woodbine, in May 1892, was a veritable beehive. On the one side of the track was the little boardinghouse of Mrs. Lipman, who was the sweetest, kindest of women. She made her hearth the fireside of every man who, in the cold evenings, had nothing but a barn to go to—cold comfort indeed after a trying day's work in the open. On the other side of the railroad, at the back of the house, was my husband's office, always crowded to capacity, in the evenings, with men who came in to be paid for work done; to have money orders sent with letters to the folks back home; or to ask all kinds of advice.

A grocery was soon opened. People would come many miles to see the new settlement; it was the talk of the county.

My husband devoted himself to his duties. He loved his work and was happy doing it. At seven in the morning he would leave for the woods with one batch of men, and his very able assistant, Mr. Schmidt, would lead away another. At twelve they would return, and at one o'clock go back to their hard labor again. At seven in the evening, when most people think of resting, Mr. Schmidt and my husband would give advice and counsel to the sixty men. It would often be nearly midnight before the last man left.

Besides all this, he began to write articles on agriculture for a newly established paper called *The Bulletin*. One of his articles appeared in the first number, and soon after its publication he received the following letter:

> My Dear Professor Sabsovich:
>
> We have read with great interest your articles on farming. We are very eager for this kind of information. We are editing 'The Farmer' here, and I promised our readers a double supply of your valuable articles on agricultural subjects.
>
> Yours,
>
> Benjamin Greenberg

Saving money for the Fund was an idea ever present with him. It took quite a while to persuade my husband that a direct entrance to the office from the street would give me some much-needed privacy, although it did not make an extravagant outlay of Fund money. The cost was about eight dollars.

Nor would he, either, spare his strength where saving for the Fund was concerned. For several months he daily walked miles and miles through the scrub pine and sand to visit the sections where the different shifts of men were cutting down trees. He would return in the evening exhausted. It also took time to convince him that the expense of a horse and buggy would be more of an economy for the Fund than a physical breakdown for him. At last he agreed and bought a horse and carriage.

His belief in the honesty of others was a reflection of his own character. It was really the first time that he had ever had to have business dealings requiring the special kind of caution necessary to cope with Yankee horse traders. But he soon had his experiences! He knew little of horses and less of horse dealers. The first one he bought nearly killed him, as well as those riding with him. He had been victimized. The horse was a high-kicking one, not fit for use. The dealer found my husband an easy mark for his game; so, after the carriage had been broken and the driver bruised badly, the horse was given away and my husband bought another.

This one, Dandy by name, was a dandy in looks and spirit; too high-spirited, indeed! Until that time it had been my husband's impression that it was the privilege of mankind only to be nervous. He very soon found out that horses have temperament too, and that Dandy had it in a very high degree. A few arms and necks were twisted in the period of Dandy's service but no greater calamity occurred. Before anything serious could happen to her owner Dandy broke her neck in a fit of fright at an approaching train. My husband had twice been fooled, because the dealers misrepresented what they sold. Without expert advice, he did not, therefore, buy horses anymore.

The plans for the farmers' houses, which had been drawn by a New York architect, were now ready. All the former carpenters, mechanics and painters who we had among our future farmers, were given preference for the work. A great many men, too, were sent by Mr. Reichow, then head of the United Hebrew Charities, to do odd jobs, such as clearing woods, pulling stumps, building and painting. The plots on which the houses were to be erected were cleared of stumps and leveled in the spring of 1891, and the building of the sixty farmhouses began. All the ordering of the materials for building was done through my husband, and here he came across for the first time what he thought was graft.

When paying the first large check, amounting to a good many thousands of dollars, for the building materials, the owner of the mill told my husband that he was entitled to a certain commission on the deal.

"Why, I am paid for my work," he answered. "What does the commission amount to?"

On being told, he asked the dealer to deduct this sum from the total cost of the materials. During the years my husband worked for the Fund, whenever this kind of an offer was made to him, and it was made by every new dealer, his answer was always the same: "Deduct my commission from the cost of the goods."

Taking account of the money laid out by him for the Fund in building the farmhouses, the little town, with its numerous factories, and the agricultural school, no mean sum was saved by him in this way. In later years the remark was sometimes made: "Professor Sabsovich must have made lots of money in Woodbine." They undoubtedly judged him by accepted business methods, not knowing that there was in him a much higher standard of honor. To him, every dollar of the Fund was a sacred trust.

Not only the businesspeople, but the farmers, too, had to be taught a lesson in this respect. The very first year that they raised any produce, whether vegetables, fruit, fowls, butter, eggs or cheese, a donation would be brought. This custom, so much in vogue in Russia, where the tenant endeavors thus to keep in the good graces of the landlord, being out of place here, where my husband was manager, was discouraged. Invariably, when any of the farmers would bring in a gift, my husband or I would ask: "How much does it cost?"

"Why, nothing," would be the usual answer.

"Didn't you work hard for it? Did it cost you nothing? We will not take anything for nothing. Either you are paid what everybody else pays you or you take it home."

And never did the same farmer try it again.

I remember that two years later, in 1897, my husband was asked to go to Canada by the Fund Committee to investigate conditions of farming there. It was a strenuous trip, lasting several weeks. His report pleased the Committee very much, and they expressed appreciation, apart from words, by sending him a check. He sent it back at once with the following letter:

My Dear Dr. Goldman:

Your favor of the 14th, with the enclosed extra

check as compensation for my report on the Hirsch Colony in Canada, was received this morning. Highly as I appreciate your commendation, I feel it inconsistent with my status as an employee of the Fund to receive extra compensation for work ordered by the Fund. I am fully satisfied with the mere appreciation of my work, not expressed in a sum of money. Therefore you will kindly take back the check sent me by Mr. A. A. Solomons.

Yours truly,

H. L. Sabsovich

I recall distinctly the answer my husband received from Dr. Goldman, the Fund's president, who had a generous heart, wonderful vision, fine constructive ability and sincere love for the work and was always a staunch supporter of whatever Prof. Sabsovich planned for the welfare of the farmers or factory employees. He wrote: "The return of the check was a source of great pleasure to me. My faith in your fine judgment in questions of integrity is upheld again."

The words may not have been exactly these, for it is about twenty-eight years since they were written, but they represent the essence of the sentiment expressed.

CHAPTER IX
BUILDING THE COLONY

The spring of 1892 rises vividly in memory. The sixty farmers are cutting off the woods, clearing the land of stumps, and assisting carpenters, bricklayers and mechanics hired in New York or Philadelphia to build their houses. Barns and other outbuildings are springing up. In a short time this waste land, stretching for miles, has been transformed as though a magic wand had been waved over it. The people on the trains passing to the watering-places and resorts—Cape May and Ocean City—during the summer months of this year could hardly believe the testimony of their eyes. What had been, a short time before, a stretch of barren, desolate pines, was changed and enlivened so that they did not recognize it. For, when they reached Woodbine, the monotonous scene blossomed into new houses, brightly painted outbuildings, surrounded, where the pines had been cut away, with crops and young orchards. Inquiring, they would be informed that the wealth of the philanthropist, Baron de Hirsch, had made all this possible.

The Committee in charge of the Fund realized from the very start that it would take several years before the farms could be made to pay and their owners enabled to draw a living from them. They realized full well that it might take a decade before the dwellers in the Ghetto, traders for generations out of sheer necessity and denied access to the soil, would become successful husbandmen.

To enable the farmers to work their lands and at the same time to make a living, it was decided to provide a place for other industries. The Baron de Hirsch Committee persuaded one manufacturer after another to move his plant from the city, agreeing to furnish the employees with homes. Thus factories were built, with great lots and large windows close to one another, so different from the dirty, dark sweatshops of New York and Philadelphia!

At first one large factory was erected, with a few dozen houses close by, and these formed the nucleus of Woodbine Village. The houses near the new plant were occupied by its managers, officers and employees; and so the first clothing factory was opened in the autumn of 1892; and all, young and old, found work there. By this time, too, the farmers and their families were comfortably settled in their farmhouses.

A crying need for a public bathhouse soon arose, for a bathroom in a house was an unheard-of luxury. About February 1893, the public bathhouse opened its doors for the use of the people of Woodbine, free of charge. It was built of brick and comprised the Russian steam and plunge baths. The Committee presented two lots to the Brotherhood for the building, and loaned them $2,000 at four per cent. to help erect it. Brick, obtained

One of Woodbine's Original Settlers with His Family

on Goodman's farm, was bought, and the colonists put up the building themselves, at their own expense. It later became the property of the whole community.

The farmhouses were heated by wood fires, so a wood-chopping and drying machine, to make kindling wood both for the use of the settlers and for sale in the markets of Philadelphia, was installed. In fact, during the first years of Woodbine, you might see at every corner countless piles of cord-wood, chopped by the pioneer workers, ready for shipment to a firm in Philadelphia.

The farmers were a mixed class and came from all parts of Russia—Courland, South Russia, Polish Russia (then) and Galicia, Austria. We had a dozen families who would be a pride to any settlement, especially the young people—intelligent, wide-awake, ambitious. To keep these, particularly, contented on the farm and in the village, some great attraction must be planned; the social side of the settler's lives must be developed. My husband realized quickly enough that it would be his duty to make life pleasant for them and their families; and at the first opportunity that afforded, our little house was made the social center.

One Sunday in May 1892, we were to entertain at dinner the members of the Baron de Hirsch Committee and their wives. It was the first time that the whole Committee had planned to come at once to Woodbine to see the work that had been done. My husband expected from fifteen to eighteen persons. Not having had much experience in entertaining so many, we ordered everything in rather large quantities, to be on the safe side.

The dinner was ready to be served when my husband, who had gone to the station to meet the visitors, returned with a telegram which said that on account of the inclement weather, the trip to Woodbine would have to be postponed. It had, indeed, been raining for the last three days. Needless to try to describe our feelings, after the efforts we had put forth to make the dinner a success, let alone the expenditure! We had, however, the satisfaction of having with us one of the members of the Board of Directors, the late Mr. Hoffman, who arrived with his son. Unaware of the Committee's change of plans, he had been in Chicago for a few days, and came to Woodbine direct on the day set for the meeting. Of course there was an abundance of food left over; so, in the evening we invited all the young folks to supper. This was the first impromptu social given them, and if the dinner did not materialize, the supper was voted a howling success.

I must also note the first wedding that took place in Woodbine. A newly arrived immigrant, a Hercules in build and strength, Glaser by name, had drifted to Woodbine looking for work. He was given employment cutting down trees and pulling up stumps. He used to work sixteen hours a day, making four or five dollars daily—then an unheard-of figure.

He took a fancy to a girl who also had come to Woodbine in search of work. Sarah, as was her name, was employed in the boarding house. Soon they were engaged, and my husband decided that their wedding, the first in Woodbine, should be a social event for the colony. A certain sum of money was allotted for the wedding feast and everybody was invited. The factory was turned into a banquet hall. Musicians from Philadelphia were hired to play the dance music, and all had a good time. Not until the early hours of the morning did the party break up and the guests bid good-bye to the happy couple.

To provide for the future of the pair, both orphans, and realizing what a wonderful worker the man was, with all the promise of a splendid future farmer if but given the chance, my husband assigned him a farm, where he and his wife settled down, raising, besides cows, poultry, vegetables and fruit, a fine crop of seven children.

Every birthday of my husband's or of any member of his family was made a pretext for an entertainment and informal dance at our little house. In later years we used the hall at our agricultural school. All the young folks were invited, refreshments were served, and everyone enjoyed a jolly evening.

An event of interest shining out as a memory among the labors and trials of early Woodbine days, a merry one chronicled by the Cape May *Gazette* of March 3, 1899—"Prof. H. L. Sabsovich's Birthday" is herewith given in the language of that paper:

> On Friday evening, February 24, the 39th anniversary of Prof. H. L. Sabsovich's birthday was merrily celebrated at his residence. The main features of the evening were a concert given by some Philadelphia artists and the music of Mr. Lippincott—which made

The Sabsovich Cottage in Woodbine

everybody dance. The pupils of the Agricultural School were represented by a committee of three, one of whom read a very well written address, which appears below. Three of the most prominent alumni of the school presented to Prof. Sabsovich a small gold locket containing their photos and an appropriate inscription. Mr. Kotinsky made the presentation speech, to which Prof. Sabsovich responded in a few touching words. While refreshments were served toasts were offered by many of the people present, Mr. Fred Schmidt acting in the capacity of toastmaster. We beg to extend our sincerest congratulations to Superintendent Sabsovich and hope that he will be spared for many years to continue his noble work.

The address was as follows:

Dear Professor: In the name of the pupils of the Baron de Hirsch Agricultural and Industrial School, we come here to extend our greetings to you on the 39th anniversary of your birthday. We take this opportunity to express some of our sentiments toward you as a man, and as the superintendent of the school. The interest that you have taken in the promotion of agriculture among our co-religionists, both by the establishment of colonies and this institution, is deserving of praise more than we can express as young men blindly seeking an occupation wherewith they may provide themselves the ability to encounter this stern world. We have been accidentally or otherwise brought in contact with this noble and your dearly cherished institution. Our ideals of the future were vague, our prospects wore the appearance of shadows, but as time wore on, as days, weeks and months were passing, the bright star of our future slowly but surely began to peer out from behind its cloudy shroud. From day to day your earnestness and goodwill, honesty of purpose and goodness of heart became more convincing; our attachment to you grew stronger and stronger, until now, although we have had but a taste of the delicacies that you have in store for us, the bonds thus created are inseparable. Like a tender father have you led us by the hand, taught us to love the beauties of which we had had no conception. Agriculture is the noblest pursuit of man, where everyone earns his bread by the sweat of his brow; an occupation that has triumphed the world over, and its existence we find now the only one that will save our race from the plague and misery that it is bound to endure in the overcrowded cities. It was with tears of sorrow that we have forsaken the unwholesome temptations of our ghettos, but it is with tears of joy and pride that we come before you to announce that you have triumphed and we are converted. Lead us and we will follow you; be our counsellor, we pray, and we will be your disciples! In us, Sir, be sure you have reached the summit of your ambition! To you, Sir, we pledge our faith and of our confidence allow not yourself to doubt!

Agriculture, farming, country-life, peace of mind and soul is the clamor of our brethren, bitterly groaning under their yoke of semi-slavery. In farming they have hoped to find reconciliation with their sufferings as exiles, but in spite of their numerous attempts and earnest efforts, they have failed again and again. Little did they know the cause of the failure or of the methods employed or knowledge required at the present day for successful farming. With lack of knowledge came lack of confidence and finally discouragement. With your keen insight into life, your love for your brethren and phenomenal foresight, you have conceived an idea that but few could have done—the instilling into the young generation love for what is noble and good, for farming life in its most attractive aspect. To establish a thorough acquaintance with nature was your bright thought. To train the bud, while yet in its early stage of development, to assume the gorgeous perfection with which nature alone can bountifully endow it. With clear perception you have resolved to lay the foundation of agricultural life among the Jews. The vigorous, healthy and enterprising young men of the race are flexible, impressionable, delighting in beauty and appreciating the wonders of nature. They will bear witness to the wisdom of the grand structure of which you have laid the foundation. In them you are laying up a store of fame for yourself that in time shall know no bound. May the Almighty grant that you may live to see the result of your beautiful teachings! May your days be prolonged to enjoy the credit reflected upon you by your present pupils! May you live to realize the blessing and honor that your nation will justly bestow upon you! May

"Rejoicing in the Law"—*Simchas Torah*

your days be as a collection of jewels scattered in your pathway, reflecting the bright joys and happinesses of your kind deeds! May the bread of helpfulness cast by you upon the waters come back to you in the form of blessing and gratitude from those nearest you now and those who will follow them!

That all the anniversaries of the day of your birth may be golden milestones upon a smooth highway of life is the earnest wish of

Your Boys

How pleasant those parties were! I might fill page after page with descriptions of the splendid times the young people had in Woodbine, owing to my husband's untiring efforts to promote the social spirit. He never thoroughly enjoyed an evening unless Woodbine colonists were with him to enjoy it also; and, on the other hand, a jollification of any sort at the home of a farmer was no jollification unless Professor Sabsovich was there to grace it, and he never disappointed them unless it was unavoidable.

As Woodbine was located only three and one-half miles from Dennisville, my husband was eager to make friends with the people there, and to bring the immigrants, in every way possible, under the good influence of our American neighbors. To make the Jewish settlers as good farmers and as good citizens as their native neighbors was his dream. Among our men, many who came from the poorest districts of Galicia and Poland were very abject and uncouth. The American villagers, most of them seeing Russian immigrants for the first time, were not favorably impressed. They judged the immigrant by his appearance, which, to tell the truth, was far from attractive, especially when we remember that, like all pioneers, his first winter was spent in a cold barn, without accommodations for a good wash, let alone a bath. But my husband worked constantly for a better understanding with the Americans.

November 5, 1892, my husband wrote to the representative of the farmers in the New York office:

> Yesterday was the first manifestation of Woodbine's political life, and it made a great impression on our American neighbors. We had a fine torch-light parade. Mr. Y. tried to buy votes, but I'll see to it that Woodbine is free of the blame of being corrupted.

CHAPTER X
THE FIRST PROBLEMS

The Woodbine settlers came into daily contact with the Dennisville people, as the village was the supply-station for the everyday needs of our colonists. All that Woodbine had at the time was one very small grocery store. The occasion of the first clash with our American neighbors was the refusal of the Dennisville barber to cut the hair of a young man, an engineer in one of the factories, who had lived in the country for several years and was quite Americanized. The barber's explanation was a threatened boycott by his clientele if he served the Jews.

Very angry, the young man came straight from the barber to my husband's office, and told him of the incident. My husband was just as indignant as he. Mr. Rice, a fine old gentleman, much respected in the village, was sent for. He had surveyed the Woodbine lands and procured much work for the Dennisville people, so that their pay-envelopes grew bigger and bigger each week through their connection with the Woodbine Land Improvement Company. My husband told him that he would be forced to discharge all the

Dennisville men we employed, unless they learned to treat our people more tolerantly.

Although the boycott was taken off at once and a number of the most representative members of the Dennisville community came over and apologized, my husband and the settlers had had their pride so deeply hurt that they knew they would never go back to that shop. When one of the settlers, who had been a barber in Russia, Mr. Shapiro, volunteered to open a shop of his own they caught at the opportunity. The right inducement was offered him, and in a few days the first barber shop was opened in Woodbine.

The Post Office had been established in the center of the village. The first Postmaster, a native American, was always complaining of the curious way in which the settlers would seal their letters, with stamps on the reverse side of the envelope. To his great disgust and annoyance the letters received from Europe would also be sealed in the same way. He asked my husband once: "Why does the Jew put his stamps on the flap of the envelope?" The answer my husband gave seemed to satisfy him.

"In Russia," he explained, "the post office clerks often tamper with and open letters coming through their hands, and to prevent this the stamp is put on the letter as a seal."

Many customs of the Jews seemed peculiar to the native, especially the demonstrative and affectionate partings. On Saturday morning, the day of rest, when the train left, the station would be black with young and old. There was great curiosity to see people go and come, and to witness affectionate embraces, often accompanied by tears, before departure. No wonder, then, that once, when I was seated in the train, a lady approached me and asked me whether all the people who were bidding such affectionate good-byes were leaving for the "other side," never to return? Her amazement was great when I told her that to my knowledge most of them were coming back on the same train that evening; though some might not return for a few days!

There were, by this time, a great many children of school age amongst us. An old two-story house on the south side of the railroad was equipped with all the necessary school furnishings, and Miss H——, a native of Dennisville, was engaged as teacher. So the first Woodbine public school came into being. A night school was opened in connection with it, to teach the older folks English, the bookkeeper in the office becoming the first instructor.

The first public school teacher had rather a hard time of it, as a number of the pupils were immigrants, newly arrived, and teacher and children spoke different languages. We might have engaged a teacher of Russian descent, with the result of enabling teacher and pupils to understand one another's speech, and simplify the work. But so earnest was my husband's desire to Americanize the youth of Woodbine and to inculcate in them the true American spirit, that only one whose forefathers were natives would satisfy him. Slowly, but surely the work of the American-born teacher took root in the minds and hearts of the little ones, who had their eyes and ears wide open to every new impression.

The Christmas holidays of 1892 approached. A few Christian families lived in Woodbine and coming in contact daily with them and the people of the surrounding villages, the Jewish children could not but be aroused to a holiday spirit as well. We had about seventy-five school-children at the time, for, besides the farmers' little ones, there were the children of the Jewish factory employees. It happened that Chanuka, the Feast of Lights, fell that year within Christmas week. So, to give our own school-children, too, a chance to enjoy a happy holiday, my husband asked our Committee to give a certain sum of money to cover the cost of the festivities. The Committee cheerfully agreed, and with one hundred dollars in my pocketbook, I went to Philadelphia and bought for each child a top, a book and a box of candy, as well as fruit and soft drinks for the older folks. So we prepared a simple entertainment. The factory was again turned into a jollification place, and the first public school entertainment by and for Woodbine school-children took place.

During the evening two of the employees in the office of the factory came up to me as the manager of the affair, and asked if they might contribute their bit to the entertainment. They were comedians, they said. Their "bit" was the great hit of the evening, and no wonder, for a few years later they appeared as headliners on Broadway with "Weber and Fields."

Early one morning the next Spring, on the first day of Pesach, my husband happened to go up to the railroad station, and while there he was handed a telegram.

I saw him stagger and turn ashen white as he read it.

"What's the trouble? What has happened?" I asked.

He handed me the telegram. It said:

> Your integrity at stake. Come to New York as soon as you can.
>
> Julius Goldman

"I am going by the next train," he said, recovering himself a little. And two hours later he left for New York in an intensely agitated state of mind. On the following day, when he returned, he told me the story.

A certain person, connected with the New York office of the Baron de Hirsch Fund, jealous of my husband's good work in Woodbine, and of his excellent standing with the Committee and the people, began by insinuation, dropping a word now and then, to try to arouse suspicion in the minds of the Committee, that something was wrong with the method in which my husband kept the books and handled the money.

By this time about $300,000 had passed through his hands. For a long time, in his zeal to economize, he had had no bookkeeper at all. Considering, therefore, the amount of construction work that had been going on in Woodbine for the farmers and the town, the long hours spent in work, and the fact that he was not a trained bookkeeper himself, it would have been remarkable, nay, miraculous if mistakes had not occurred. But whenever, in his monthly reports, the accounts did not agree, he had always made good out of his own salary.

To put an end to this malicious rumor, my husband asked Dr. Goldman to send an expert auditor to Woodbine, and in a few weeks Mr. A. S. Solomons came down. He was the general agent of the Fund at that time. It may be mentioned here that Mr. Solomons was one of the founders, with Miss Clara Barton, of the American Red Cross, September 1, 1882, at Washington, D. C., and was conspicuously instrumental in organizing this greatest of humanitarian bodies along lines of practical effectiveness.

He worked five days over the books, checking up minutely every voucher, and, at the end of the week, telegraphed the President of the Committee that the books were in splendid shape, and that the Committee might be congratulated on having Professor Sabsovich's sterling abilities at their command.

The man responsible for the rumors was requested to resign and that severed his connection with the Fund forever.

Dr. Goldman hastened to assure my husband that his honesty had never been doubted for an instant by him, but that there had been in existence a persistent undercurrent of complaint that the books were not being properly kept, and he wished to silence it at once and for all. A letter of my husband's, written to Dr. Goldman at that time reads as follows:

> I shall be glad to get rid of all accounts, bookkeeping, etc. It wearies me more than any of the work outdoors. When the work in the fields starts, and

everything goes smoothly, as I hope it will, you'll not recognize me. Good spirits and hope for the success of our undertaking will do me far more good than any amount of caring for my physical health ever will.

(Dr. Goldman had expressed his anxiety about the state of my husband's health.)

Of the good friends made among his colleagues while on the staff of the Fort Collins Agricultural College, he had corresponded regularly with one who, by 1892, had become Director of the Lincoln Agricultural College in Nebraska. Professor Ingersoll had heard of the great hardships my husband had been enduring in furthering to his utmost the welfare of the new colony, and he wrote to summon him to Nebraska to work at Lincoln. Here is the letter my husband wrote to Professor Ingersoll in answer to the invitation:

Dear Friend

Your valuable and friendly letter of Nov. 28th is at hand. I appreciate your warm feeling toward me and your splendid offer. The troubles I have had with my co-workers were settled in the spring. Now I am directly responsible to the Directors of our Fund.

The results of the first agricultural season are more favorable than I had expected, considering all the difficulties we had to overcome. You know from my previous letters that our place is adapted to fruit growing and market gardening. Out of sixty orchards planted, only in a half-dozen is the percentage of dead trees about five per cent. With small fruits we have had the same result. While raising fruit, we have also been successful with watermelon culture, early potatoes, sweet potatoes and cucumbers. It seems our soil and climate are well adapted to growing these vegetables. On account of the late planting, and the fact that I did not have a chance to prepare the land right, I was not successful in raising strawberries. . . .

Concerning the industries, the Fund has built two factories, which employ 180 hands and are able to employ 100 more. As the farming population cannot supply enough hands for the factories, the Fund has built 22 nice cottages, costing $1000 to $1500 each, and a pleasant hotel, heated by steam and lighted by electricity.

I have graded four miles of farm roads 25 feet wide, and over two miles of streets and avenues in town, 66 to 100 feet wide. 67 farms are under cultivation; that is, about 700 acres. 200 acres are cleared in town and 100 acres of roads. By increasing the number of factories we expect to increase the town population, and in this way to create a local market for the farm surplus.

Our educational facilities are yet small, but we have opened two temporary schools with an attendance of 100 children and also a night school for adults with 25 to 30 in attendance. I and my new co-worker, Arthur Reichow, are trying to induce the Fund to build a central education institution, where manual training and improved scientific and agricultural studies will be connected with public education; that is, to create a "People's University." This would be practicable,

The Founder of the Colony Personally Supervising the Building of Settler's Cottage

since the State will be willing to bear one-half of the expense in starting and supporting such an institution. The State of New Jersey is very liberal in this direction. I am only sorry that the people do not all make use, as yet, of the liberal support offered to them by their State. You see, my friend, what a really wonderful field for splendid work there is here for me in every line, every direction. But in case my work is not appreciated, as it often happens that sincere and earnest workers do not succeed in accomplishing what is so dear to them, and if I am compelled to seek another field of activity, I shall look forward to working with you. But I would then, and only then, consider your kind offer.

Yours,
H. L. Sabsovich

Very soon after, in February 1893, my husband, the idea seeming to have taken hold of him, wrote on the subject of the "People's University" to Judge Meyer Isaacs, then President of the Fund.

My Dear Judge:

I am so glad that you are considering an industrial and agricultural school in connection with the public school. If I am not mistaken, Woodbine would be the first place in this State where public education would be carried on upon such an improved basis. From the lowest grades up our children will be taught to become useful and self-supporting members of the community. An agricultural education is the more necessary for them, who have not the inherited sentiments of the farmer's son, which often saves him for the rural life. We have to implant an industrial and agricultural spirit in our children, and this will take from our race some of the blame we are subjected to in the world. Many western agricultural colleges have introduced a system of paying five to ten cents an hour for work in the fields or in the shop, in order to enable the boys and girls to earn a little money, and thus partly lift the burden from the parents' shoulders during their schooling. If we introduce such a system into our schools, we shall save our girls of thirteen and fourteen years of age from the factories, inasmuch as they will earn $1.50 to $2.50 a week, an amount large enough to pay their parents for their board. Especially in field and garden work we may expect some returns.

A few months later he wrote to Dr. Julius Goldman on the same subject, and, among other things, says:

Farming is becoming an art and a science, and I do not doubt that our government will soon see that secondary schools should have agricultural and industrial departments.

In another letter he writes:

I have received a copy of a Trenton paper (*The Daily State Gazette*) which I send you by this mail. You will find there the article: "The Farmers in Session," and you will see the one point I am after, and which I have been advocating lately: teaching agriculture in public schools—is earnestly discussed.

He was ever reluctant to engage any personal friend to work in Woodbine, fearing misunderstandings and the breaking of friendship. One Summer day I happened to be in New York and found that an old friend of ours who had been a high school teacher on the other side, was in New York with his family. I went at once to see them and found them in terrible straits, all their money nearly gone, the friend's eyesight badly affected, and he in poor health. His health would be assured, I was told, if he could work in the country somewhere. I returned next day to Woodbine, and told my husband of the meeting.

"Why," he said, "I am in a position to help him at once, as I am badly in need of a teacher of mathematics." This was exactly the position he had occupied in the high school on the other side. My husband wrote to him to come, which he did. For about two years he was a teacher in the loft above the barn, which had been turned into the Agricultural School.

One day he told my husband that he was eager to go back to the old country, but that he did not have any savings. He asked my husband to keep him on the payroll for two or three months after he left, to tide him over. This was flatly refused. My husband said that under no circumstances would he do a thing like that. Not only did the friendship break, but the man, at a banquet tendered him by his New York friends on the occasion of his departure, vilified my husband. Our dear friend Kaplan, who attended the banquet, arose and told the guests that he knew the merits of the case better, and would not allow a man's name to be slandered who was blameless, especially when not there to defend himself.

And this was only one of numerous cases where sincere devotion to inborn high standards in work was his unfailing guide, even at the risk of jeopardizing life-long friendships.

CHAPTER XI
UNREST AMONG THE COLONISTS

But a serious trouble, not destined to be so lightly met and settled, was brewing for my husband. Under the leadership of a person whose main joy in life was meddling, the farmers conferred and decided they would not pay the interest due the Fund, although, when applying for farming land, each of them had signed a paper agreeing, in ten years' time, to return every cent loaned him, with interest. The conditions had been made very clear to them—every angle of the transaction having been explained.

When my husband was confronted with this refusal of the farmers to pay the amount due, he was exceedingly indignant. He was unable to view the matter from their viewpoint at all. Being a man always ready to give, but reluctant to take, he tried to show them that their stand in the matter revealed a lack of pride and dignity. He told them he could not conceive how they could wish to obtain something for nothing; especially as it had been a clear business deal between the Fund and the farmer from the beginning. The well-defined position of Baron de Hirsch, who donated the money, and the Committee administering it, had been from the start that of loaning means for every applicant to make a beginning as a farmer. He recalled to the men the point of honor made by the very first Jews arriving in the American Colonies, when they vowed never to allow any one of their number to become a public charge, never to accept charity.

My husband told them that he had too much respect for Jews to think of the colonists assuming, at that late day, any other position. It hurt him, he explained, that the men he had always fought for so consistently, should have assumed this strange attitude. He always had felt especially happy when he had been able to convince the Committee on other occasions that the farmers were in the right, for he had been thoroughly in sympathy with them and their families in the time when they were undergoing hardships in their pioneer life in Woodbine, and he begged them to consider the matter in the true and righteous light of honest men.

Anxious to act, as always, as clear-headed mediator in his trying position, he had written to Dr. Goldman under date of March 1, 1893, before the trouble over interest payments.

I strongly advocate more help for the farmers. I would suggest that we advance them $100 each to plow and harrow the land; for, though they earned good money during the first year of Woodbine's existence, still, considering that everyone had to build a new home, and besides that, send a considerable amount of money to Russia to bring their families over, and to invest some on their farms, it is easy to realize that of their earnings they could save nothing. By helping them to improve their farms we shall the sooner free them from our wardship. After all, they are our wards!

But, in their refusal to pay their interest to the Fund my husband could not and would not take sides with them, and a hard struggle began.

In the simplicity of character which was his, he could show strength when it was demanded. He knew that he stood for the right and that it would prevail in the end. He felt that the farmers were, for the time being, blinded to the truth.

The fight thus begun lasted over a year. The farmers demanded the deeds for their lands, which they had refused to pay for, making the claim that Baron de Hirsch had intended the farms as gifts, not loans. (Baron de Hirsch had died shortly before the dispute began.)

My husband tried to make the farmers understand that their plan would take the form of charity dispensed to them, but they could not see it in that way.

The meddler, before mentioned, who had originally come to Woodbine as a worker in the pay of the Committee, began to play on their lower instincts. His scheming, like that of all his kind, was underhanded and trouble soon developed of an alarming nature. The farmers stopped working their land, and meeting secretly day and night and conspiring, threatened to kill my husband and burn his home. They ceased to greet him civilly, or even speak to him unless business necessitated and compelled them to go to his office. Young and old showed the greatest animosity, and although they did not know the meaning of the word "boycott," that was, in fact, what it amounted to.

In explanation my husband wrote to Mr. Reichow, regarding this phase of the struggle:

> I am just sick at heart! It is easy for you in New York to philosophize; but here I am, face to face with indignities, insults, sour remarks. These last two days here I can never forget. I tremble all over—I cannot think—my mind is in a whirl. I have had more excitement than I can endure.

A few days later he again wrote:

> What reasonable human good can you expect from people who are risking their own welfare and that of their families simply because someone has told them that the leases are no good? They want to see the Committee; especially Mr. Jacob Schiff and Mr. Jesse Seligman, in whom they say they "have the utmost confidence." The most reasonable demand the farmers make is that the time be extended from fifteen to twenty-four years, with no interest whatsoever. I can see where the extension of time might be granted. I often wonder whether they are children or fools, or both together?

In another letter, to Mr. Reichow, he says:

ARTHUR REICHOW

DR. PAUL KAPLAN

Two of Woodbine's Best Friends

A reporter sent by Mr. Goodale has come on behalf of the farmers. It seems to me this reporter does not care to find out the truth; he only wants to arouse public opinion favorable to the agitating farmers. I know that their case will be lost when brought before a court (and to keep out of court is the farmers' aim); but I see disaster for Woodbine if legal proceedings are not taken up.

In a letter to Dr. Goldman, he says:

We must take decided action. Soon the public will know the truth—that the settlers want to become owners of the farms without paying for them.

Ten days later he wrote Mr. Reichow:

I am trying to bury my feelings, trying to be calm, but it costs me my health. I feel so uneasy every time I have to leave Woodbine on business that I shall have heart failure. I begin to lose courage. I am afraid I am becoming quixotic. Threats are being made openly, and I am warned by several outsiders to be cautious. I do not pay much attention to these threats, but my family is very much worried about me. I would perhaps resign, but not until I see justice done, even if my life is in danger.

To Mr. Jacob Schiff, April 18, he wrote:

My dear Mr. Schiff:

I thank you so much for your confidence and the support you give me in our just fight with the farmers here. Let us hope that daylight will soon break, peace and order be restored, and the quiet development of our community be uninterrupted.

A few days later in a ten-page letter to Dr. Goldman, he said, among other things:

I have experienced another grave disappointment. I called a meeting of all the farmers in the factory, and showed them how ridiculous and unjust their demands are, how ruinous it will be to them to cling to their ring-leaders (and all the ring-leaders were present on the occasion). I came to them ready to forgive and forget all, eager only to create a golden bridge of reconciliation, bringing words of harmony. Instead of taking my advances in the true spirit, their ring-leaders explained my move as weakness. I am afraid now that only by exercising our rights to the full extent shall we move them from this demoralizing and misleading stand of theirs.

The trouble-maker sent one article after another to the press, depicting my husband as the "man ruling Woodbine like the Czar of Russia." We all know that even the best of men have enemies who prick up their ears, ready to listen to the charges of a scandalmonger. My husband never replied to these attacks. He felt that he was above such slander. Several newspapers offered, for certain sums of money, to publish favorable reports of him and of his work. He closed his door on their agents as an answer.

My husband still labored in the interest of the farmers, having to deal with jealousies that arose not only among co-workers, as in the rumor of careless book-keeping, but from other sources as well. The stubborn dissatisfaction of the farmers hurt him intensely, since he knew it was so ill-founded. From the day that he came to Woodbine he had always had to battle, sometimes on behalf of the farmers, sometimes his own. But now, receiving one shock after another, the accumulation of anxieties seriously affected his health. The breakdown came very suddenly one night in December 1893.

We had been visiting dear friends in the village, and, on our way home, he collapsed suddenly in the street. Mrs. Lipman and I carried him to the nearest house. It was then midnight. We sent for a doctor, who, upon examining him, shook his head gravely. He was moved the next morning to his own home, where, for two months, he lay dangerously ill. As soon as he was able to leave his bed, the physician advised a sojourn in a warmer climate, for it was a very cold February. As he was simply convalescent, he could not safely travel alone, so his eldest daughter, Marie, went with him. She was not yet eight, but a most capable little woman and devoted nurse. They spent six weeks in Florida, where he recovered his strength. Returning, he felt quite himself again, as he resumed his work.

The disputes and differences with the farmers had not been settled, and daily he had to meet and deal with them and to sense their unchanged animosity. Very soon, too, trouble started in the factory. He was always the arbitrator of disputes between employer and worker, and he put every effort into a settlement of the grievances of the working people, but aggravation followed upon aggravation, and at the end of May he had a relapse. His life, even, was despaired of.

For two long months there was a race between life and death. Having always been a man of the most temperate habits, life for the second time won the race. In his convalescent period he went to a boarding house in the Catskills, kept by Mrs. Augusta Lenson, and she and her charming daughters gave him such wonderful care, that the summer spent there wrought a miracle. He left us a bundle of bones scarcely covered with flesh, and returned a man in the full flush of health. By the end of August he had gained thirty-five pounds. He began to broaden out, the hollows of his cheeks filled, and he looked the picture of health. How he changed after this severe illness may be illustrated by this interesting incident. In 1889, our first year in New York, he had received a letter from a friend of his, a chemist in Odessa, asking him to find out the prices of certain chemicals. This made it necessary for him to go to the Stock Exchange. He never knew how he did it, but he reached a certain window inside the Exchange. In his broken speech he asked a few questions. The man at the window very angrily inquired how he had gained admittance. Not having the least idea that there was a sanctum sanctorum there, where not every mortal could be admitted, he replied, simply: "Why, nobody stopped me!"

Then the man looking at him more keenly, began to smile, and said: "No wonder! You are the image of Jay Gould and our new doorkeeper must have taken you for him."

But in later years, people, on seeing him, would often remark that they had never seen a more striking resemblance to Gen. U. S. Grant. Never having seen either Jay Gould or Gen. Grant, he was greatly amused that at different periods of his life he had been thought to resemble, in feature, two men so widely different from each other and from himself.

While my husband was staying in the Catskills with his oldest daughter, a fourth daughter was born to him. He was very fond of Dr. Julius Goldman, and had been hoping for a chance to name a son for him; but the boy disappointed him by turning out to be a girl. So the best we could do was to call her Julia.

September 1893 came, and still the farmers were obdurate. My husband tried to make them realize how ruinous their attitude was. They had not tilled their fields that Spring, and a whole year's crops were lost. He assured them that neither in a court of law, nor in a court of arbitration would their case ever stand a test, as it had no moral nor legal justification; but they were deaf to all remonstrance and dead to reason, and in November they entered a suit against the Baron de

Hirsch Fund. The case was heard at the Cape May Court House—Dr. Goldman, Judge Isaacs and my husband representing the Fund.

The judge before whom the case came for trial found no cause for action in the farmer's complaint. With but slight consideration he dismissed the case, stating that there was not then nor ever had been any moral nor legal ground for action.

The farmers were apparently astounded at the prompt adverse decision. For a whole year the Committee and my husband had been unable to induce the farmers to sense that which the court, in its official capacity, had caused them to realize in half an hour. When my husband left the courtroom, he found the farmers gathered in an indeterminate group, apparently too astonished to decide what to do next. It occurred to him that, having had so many things to do in Woodbine, he might have overlooked some just cause for dissatisfaction.

So, with this thought in mind, he approached them. He ignored all past insults, all former animosity, and passing over what very few men would have done, invited them to his home with these words: "The law has decided against you, but bring me your old leases, and we will see if we cannot, in a mutual spirit of kindliness, do better than you alone could do in a state of anger."

That night the farmers gathered at the house, and great was their amazement to find that the man whom they had tormented, whose home they had threatened to mob and burn, was as ready to concede their just claims, as of old. My husband had prevailed upon the

Committee to make some important concessions in the leases, and when they were explained it was a different group of farmers who left the house.

"Now that we understand one another," said my husband, "we shall get along," and with renewed confidence on each side they parted.

Never was there a happier man than my husband that night. The farmers' hearts were won back to him, and from that time there was no doubt in their minds that his heart was wholly theirs; that he cared for each, individually, and that in time of trouble they could be sure of receiving all the sympathy for which they had need.

My husband was a man of vision and large dreams. He felt and knew that, with peace in sight, constructive work for Woodbine would begin again. Many plans for the good of the colonists were in his mind and one enterprise after another was suggested to the Fund Committee, as he knew that the public-spirited group of New York and Philadelphia men who made up the Baron de Hirsch Fund Committee was more than anxious to see the colonists prosper.

A dispute presently arose between the manufacturers and the working people regarding the Sabbath rest. The manufacturers, for purely economic reasons, wanted Sunday as the day of rest. The working people, many of them orthodox Jews, insisted on Saturday as their Sabbath. My husband was not orthodox himself. To the services of the synagogue he had never been drawn, because it was for him only a splendid tradition. His religion was the brotherhood of man. But he clearly sensed the viewpoint of the people and brought all his influence to bear to obtain a ruling that in the colony whistles should not call the people to work on the sixth day of the week. And to this day Saturday is the day of rest in Woodbine.

CHAPTER XII
ADDED INDUSTRIES

More factories were erected; more houses sprang up in the little village. The first needle factory changed hands several times until Mr. Rabinovich took charge of it. Twenty-four years before he had come out as the manager of the largest factory, and is today the owner of the largest plant in Woodbine. During the World War as many as eight hundred people were engaged in his clothing factory, making war supplies. Needless to say that, coming to Woodbine a very poor man, he is today very rich.

A machine plant was also started by Morris L. Bayard, who, as a poor laborer, at first dug the wells and set the pumps for the Woodbine farms and town homes. He had then only a small supply shop, a shanty eight feet by ten, but through the years he has become the most prosperous man, not only in Woodbine, but in the whole county. He was always keenly alive to every opportunity, and my husband often remarked that it was a pleasure to help a man like that.

"Give him one push," he would often say when other mechanics thought he was partial to Bayard in awarding contracts, "and he flies so far that it is hard to catch him."

A tool factory was opened, a basket factory—which lasted only a few years—a knitting mill and a hat factory. Some of these concerns are working there today; some have changed hands and removed.

Several dozen five-room houses were built around them and the ensemble made up the industrial center of Woodbine. The Baron de Hirsch Fund built the houses, gave them to the tenants on a first mortgage, and by paying eight dollars a month each man became, in eight or ten years, the owner of his little dwelling. Remembering that these people had come from either the pale of settlement in Russia, where they had existed in utter poverty; or from the slums of New York or Philadelphia, where a whole grown family would be crowded into two or three rooms, it may be imagined that this bright, cheerful, sunny, little house, set on a large plot of ground, appeared to them a veritable paradise.

My husband's interest in the workingmen's cause brought him into difficulties. The manufacturers said that, owing to his "interference," the workingmen were leaving them. In answer to this charge, he wrote:

> You know, my dear Mr. Reichow, as well as I do, that it is the higher wages that workingmen earn in other places; that, and only that causes the migration of the employee—not Sabsovich.

The economic depression of 1893 affected the cloak industry unfavorably and the decreased demand led to a partial suspension of work in the Woodbine factory. The discontent among the workers and the strikes that followed caused the plant to shut down entirely. Many farmers left, unable to earn a living either from their land or in the factory. Those who remained were given work cutting wood, pulling stumps or clearing the town land to make streets. Some picked huckleberries and some worked in the canning factory nearby. In pursuing this course my husband anticipated a method of dealing with the problem of unemployment, which has since been widely discussed, but only here and there put into action.

By 1894–95, however, the outlook became brighter with the opening of another factory. After that a few other plants were established and the little place steadily grew in population.

CHAPTER XIII
STRENGTHENING THE NEW ALLEGIANCE

The little village at this period presented a very pretty appearance. The streets were lined with two rows of poplars, which had grown so richly that in Summer they afforded perfect shade. Grass-plots bordering the sidewalks added to the fresh beauty and repose of the scene. In fact, Woodbine then became really a large park. It was, however, much more than simply ornamental. It had grown into a good-sized village, several new stores—grocery, dry goods, shoe and hardware—having recently been opened.

But, attractive as the village was, my husband had plans to improve it still further. He was invited to address one of the Saturday afternoon women's meetings, and, amongst other plans, announced on that occasion his intention of offering prizes for the cleanest and best-looking house fronts and yards; remarking that he was ready to supply, free, all the plants and flowers any dweller wished to use. That set the ball rolling. Each family tried to outdo the other in making the prettiest showing, and the result more than justified his hopes. From that season on, Woodbine has each successive Summer resolved into a veritable flower-garden of beauty and fragrance.

In 1892 the first schoolhouse was built at one end of the farm settlement. Two years later the need for another arose, and this was erected at the opposite end of the town. Several years later still another school was built in the center of the village itself. A kindergarten, the very first to open in Cape May County—settled for over two hundred years—was started and conducted by a very intelligent, wide-awake girl, whose work was quickly appreciated by the parents of the children. Only teachers of the highest standing available were considered for the school service, and with its splendid group of instructors and bright, ambitious pupils, Woodbine soon had reason to be proud of the showing at the county commencement, where the girls and boys received the official meed of highest merit. With such activities as public lectures and frequent entertainments of an intellectual character, Woodbine rapidly became the center of the county's mental activity.

My husband was an enthusiast for Americanization, as he fully appreciated the difference between the institutions and conditions our colonists lived—or, rather, suffered under—in the places they came from abroad, and the conditions and institutions they were fortunate enough to enjoy in this country. Not an Independence Day, or a Washington's or Lincoln's Birthday passed unnoticed. In fact, the utmost care was taken to have the best speakers from New York and Philadelphia as guests for these occasions. The school teachers would

The Growing Colony

prepare an ambitious school entertainment and the significance of the day was touched upon from every possible angle. The celebration would begin in the morning at the schoolhouse and end at night in the big hall, with speeches and dancing.

Educational work in Woodbine was so active that my husband could not bear to have anything interfere with its progress. On one occasion, August 1904, he wrote this letter to the School Board of Dennis Township:

Sirs:

The new district law has deprived us of home rule. For us in Woodbine educational facilities are of a very vital character. The conduct of educational matters in Woodbine is carried on by a Board consisting of the trustees of two school districts, the teachers and myself. Often the parents are called in to aid the board and teacher in improving the behavior, manners or general appearance of the children. The board tries to interest the parents in school matters; tries to bring forward the spirit of American principles and inculcate American patriotism through the children into the homes.

This explains why we felt alarmed when we learned about the new Townships School Act, passed by our legislators in the interest of the Republican principles of concentration of power to the detriment of Democratic principles of home rule. Therefore we welcome your apparent desire to help us to return to home rule in Woodbine school management.

He also said in this letter: "Manual training and physical culture in the public schools should be the first step toward developing a sound mind in a sound body."

This will show that his ideas on education were several decades ahead of time.

While on the subject of the public schools of Woodbine I must not neglect to relate what happened in connection with the large Central School, the fourth one built. For a few years my husband had felt that Woodbine was large enough to have a graded school, also a high school in the center of the village. By this time we had a number of boys and girls, graduated from public school, attending Millville High School, twenty-five miles away. This bi-daily trip was quite a strain upon the students, and my husband felt it should be spared them. There were, besides, other children rapidly growing up to high school age. The township, he knew, would share the cost of the building and upkeep of such a school; but it would mean a somewhat heavier taxation for the Woodbine people. The same troublemaker who had figured in the farmers' strike began to prejudice the people against such a project, bringing forward the argument that this would mean a financial burden for them in extra taxation. The appropriation of funds for the building of this educational center and high school would have, of course, to be voted upon by the citizens of Woodbine. My husband was so thoroughly convinced of the great need for such a school that, to make sure that it would not be outvoted by the hostile forces—working in the dark and led by the man who never played fair—he called all the women to be present at a meeting. (In New Jersey, women had the right to vote on school appropriations—partial suffrage.) He explained the situation to them, and when the day for voting the school appropriations came, not a woman remained at home, and the resolution for the building of the Central School was carried by an overwhelming majority.

In 1903 the school was built and it is not only the pride of Woodbine, but of the county, the people of which send many a boy and girl to it. Woodbine High School was the stepping-stone of many ambitious young folks to a fundamental education and a larger life. All those who had been misled to vote against the appropriation for the school realized their mistake in the years that followed, and felt abashed when they came to witness the graduation of their own offspring and sensed the splendid results achieved by them.

Two years after the school was built the School Board felt that a fence which might cost about $400 or $500 was needed for it. My husband called a meeting of all the Woodbine settlers and laid the plan before them. It was decided that an entertainment in the large hall of the Central High School would be an effective way of raising the funds. Though some people thought that Woodbine could not raise more than a hundred dollars, they lost out in their surmise, for the full amount was collected, and never did I see a more enthusiastic gathering, nor one more ready to spend freely.

The dedication of the Central High School took place on Columbus Day, 1905. About five hundred

Woodbine's Best Crop

children gathered in the assembly room, entering four by four, headed by their teachers, where they participated in a program of patriotic exercises. The building, which was crowded with people, inside and out, was decorated with American flags.

The program started with the "Star-Spangled Banner," followed by "The Flag of the Free." Patriotic speeches were delivered by some of the specially invited guests and by my husband, who always reached the hearts of young and old quickly with sincere and earnest words. Mr. A. S. Solomons, who graced every grand occasion in Woodbine, and in whom Americanization of the immigrant boys and girls had a staunch supporter, presided at the exercises. Old Glory was unfurled, and as it floated over the beautiful white head of this venerable man, he raised his hand and the five hundred children, looking straight at him, recited clearly and strongly:

> Flag of our great republic! Inspirer of battle! Guardian of our homes! Whose stars and stripes stand for truth, bravery, purity and union, we salute thee! We, the children of distant lands, who find rest beneath thy folds, do pledge ourselves, our hearts, our sacred honor, to love and protect thee, our country and the liberty of the American people forever!

The enthusiasm of the people assembled knew no bounds and the walls rang with cheers.

My husband was imbued with a truly democratic spirit. He met everyone on a footing of equality, with the simplicity of a truly good nature unburdened by conventional prejudices. One of the yearly Teachers' Institutes was held in Woodbine. Among the assembled teachers was a colored woman. During the session she read an extremely interesting paper on education, and had taken an active part in the discussion that followed. My husband acted as host. He invited the association to meet in Woodbine, and, as a special courtesy, ordered a dinner at the hotel and summoned them all. When the guests had been seated, himself at the head of the table with the president of the association, a Southerner, at his right hand, he noticed that the colored teacher was not with them. Leaving his place, he went in search of her, and came upon her in one of the adjoining rooms opening a dinner-basket. In answer to his inquiry why she had not availed herself of his invitation to dinner, she said that, as a colored woman, she thought she was not included. He immediately escorted her to the table and placed her beside himself, on the left. He remained quite indifferent to the storm of criticism evoked from the President and a few others who entertained the same prejudices.

CHAPTER XIV
BRINGING SCIENCE TO THE FARMERS

If my husband was interested in public schools and in the subject of general education in Woodbine, he was even more deeply devoted to the task of providing agricultural training for the young sons of the farmers, and so teaching them to grow up good farmers themselves. From the very first he had felt that the success of the colony would depend upon the theoretical instruction, as well as the practical guidance that the farmers would get. The latter they must have, of course. They would be shown *how* to do things. But, as he was well aware, the Jewish mind is ever busy with the "why and wherefore" of moves and actions. If his queries cannot be convincingly answered, his interest cannot be firmly held.

Here was a group of ex-tailors, ex-shoemakers, ex-peddlers and ex-sewing-machine operators. Their minds had developed along certain lines of skill and shrewdness; and if these men were to become good farmers, their minds must be nourished and satisfied while their unused muscles were being trained. Each man must be made to understand *why* it was good to be a farmer, apart from mere self-interest, *wherein* work with the soil is satisfying; and *how* a man can overcome the handicaps and trials Nature imposes on him on the road to successful husbandry. The native farmer, whose family has lived on the land for many generations, has grown up with this knowledge. The love of the soil is in his veins, and that is what makes him keep to the farm in spite of discouragements. My husband felt that this entire farming tradition must be built up if Woodbine colonists were to become and remain the equals of the native farmers. Therefore he intended that the colonists should be instructed in every branch of the theoretical and practical knowledge that would make for a farmer's success. Not only this, but he meant to bring up the sons of the farmers, from the beginning, to understand and love the work on a farm.

We had tried to develop the social side of life in Woodbine so that the young folks might have an outlet for their natural love of fun. There should be nothing of the dull, uninviting farm life about our Woodbine Colony! And my husband worked constantly, as I have shown, to have so many schools and such good schools in Woodbine that the growing minds of the youngsters would find ample food and opportunity for growth. Now he felt he could turn to the job that interested him most of all. He was going to build up a thorough system of agricultural education that should develop the best material among the farmers' sons; that should cultivate professional ambition among the boys, and show them— to quote my husband's own words—"how, by the aid of science and the practical experience of other farmers, to make farming as profitable as other professions are."

Professor and Mrs. Sabsovich Entertaining at Tea

This compelling dream of his had to take shape with a small beginning. As soon as the colony was well established, my husband began a series of weekly conferences, to which the farmers and their grown-up sons were invited. Every Saturday afternoon they would meet in the hall of the village to receive instruction in farming, and to talk over their plans and the results of their work. These lectures were given in the form of explanation and comment on stereopticon views. This proved to be a good method of giving theoretical instruction to men, who, although their minds were active, were not used to getting information from lecture or textbooks. As my husband said in one of his reports:

> As we are dealing with a class of people who know little of the English language and are not otherwise prepared for mental work requiring concentration, the method to be used should be picture teaching, or addressing the mind through the instrumentality of the eye, that is, teaching by illustration. The practical training in the different kinds of work in the field and garden and orchard can go on together with an explanation in these picture talks of the anatomy of plants and trees, etc., and the best methods of feeding cattle, dairying and raising poultry. I shall also have demonstrations of the newest machines for tilling the soil, incubation and dairy-work. These lectures we want to make so attractive that our American neighbors will become interested in them, too. I am planning to show with the magic lantern pictures that are both useful and

The Original Agricultural School Had More Spirit Than Body

interesting—specimens to illustrate the construction of a leaf, the circulation of food in an animal's body, the nature of fungi, and of insects attacking our plants.

He put both of these plans for the theoretical and practical instruction of the farmers into action, and the Saturday afternoon lectures proved so beneficial that it was decided to build a large barn on Farm No. 60, the upper story of which was to be used as a lecture room. But while in course of construction the plan of the upper hall was changed, and built so as to make it available for school purposes. This was the first home of the Baron de Hirsch Agricultural School.

During the preparatory period of the school (March to October 1894) forty-two pupils were registered. The Woodbine farmers sent their sons, and so did Alliance, Carmel, Rosenhayn—the neighboring South Jersey colonies—and Jewish farmers all over the country. The first students could not receive a systematic course of lectures, as the school was not yet fully organized, but they were given practical instruction in the planting, grafting and care of fruit trees and in the growing of garden truck and field crops. Meanwhile the Model Farm did much to advance the knowledge of the farmers in general, to whom the country, soil and climate conditions were unknown when they came from their ghettos—whether in the cities of the old world or New York or Philadelphia.

It may be interesting to mention here, as an example of my husband's care for the individual students as well as the general welfare of all collectively, the case of two young boys, the sons of Woodbine farmers. They were unusually bright and intelligent and he realized that all they needed was a chance. He saw in them good teachers and future farm-inspectors, who would be all the more useful because they spoke the language of the Jewish farmers. He did not purpose to keep them waiting until the Agricultural School should grow up to their needs. He devised, therefore, a plan for their training and the Fund gave him permission to carry it out.

Shortly after peace had been made with the farmers, he called the two boys in one day, and asked them whether they would like to go to college. It was, in effect, the same as asking them whether they would like to live in bright sunshine or deep darkness! It was, of course, the dream of their young lives! But, they explained, they could not become a burden to their families, whom they were trying to support. My husband then revealed his plan. They should work two or three hours each day clearing bushes and stumps from Farm No. 60, earning pay enough to maintain themselves, and the rest of the day they might study to prepare themselves for college. The two boys were given lessons in English, with a few others, and once a week lectures on various subjects in agriculture. In eight months the two were ready for the Rutgers College entrance examinations, and, after attending for four years, they both graduated with the highest honors. Today they are scientists, one of them being of international reputation—the greatest authority on soil analysis—Dr. Jacob G. Lipman. The establishment of the Agricultural School and the scholarships meant that the Fund stood ready to do as much for any other promising pupil.

The classes in the new Agricultural School went ahead. The natural sciences—subjects such as botany, chemistry and physiology—were taught by my husband. Specialized branches of agriculture, such as poultry raising, bee-keeping and dairying were taught by Frederick Schmidt his assistant; while the general subjects, including drawing, were supervised by an alumnus, Jacob Kotinsky, of Rutgers College. Five hours were devoted to school work, and not less than five to farm work. Everything went well. The exhibits of farm products and the results of the school work at the county fair at the Court House, the Jewish Fair in Philadelphia, and the National Poultry Fair in Washington, D. C., furnished proof of the efficacy of the instruction.

The school, at this time, had more spirit than body. There were, as yet, no dormitories, and the pupils either lived with their parents or boarded in the families of the colonists.

Campus of the Baron de Hirsch Agricultural School

CHAPTER XV
A PIONEER OF AGRICULTURAL SCHOOLS

The real school was organized three years later. In 1897 large dormitories, with spacious bedrooms, assembly rooms, reading and dining rooms, were built on Farm No. 62, and a large brick school building was erected, with all kinds of laboratories. A matron, cook and other workers were employed to take care of the physical needs of the one hundred boys, and also a governor and staff of teachers in general and agricultural branches. A teachers' cottage was built on the same grounds, so that a little colony within a colony was made.

The students were trained in practical work including the raising of crops, caring for the live-stock, working in the dairy, the apiary, the hothouse, the nursery and the shops. The apiary was a special feature. It was located in the center of the orchard, and the honey which the bees produced was the finest in New Jersey. In the mechanical shop a little of blacksmithing, plumbing, carpentry, medicine and veterinary surgery were taught. This was designed to make the prospective farmer equal to any need or emergency that might arise on his farm. Nor was the marketing side of the farmer's work neglected. In the poultry plant the students were taught how to use incubators, and the method of packing poultry for market. The newest of agricultural implements—mechanical ploughs, seeders, reapers and binders—were used by the boys of the school. In fact, so complete was the equipment, that a miniature weather bureau was fitted up on the top of the fifty-foot tower in the center of the Agricultural School grounds. This had all the necessary instruments, and the students took daily observations.

The order of the school day was thus: The boys would rise at 6:30, take a cold shower, dress and start their daily work. They were led about the farm, which covered 300 acres, absorbing from actual experience knowledge of the cultivation of orchards, vineyards and greenhouses, and of the care of live-stock. Then, at ten, the day's toil was over, and the bell called all to bed and to rest.

Students of both sexes were admitted to the Agricultural School. I remember the incident which led to the opening of a department therein for girls. One afternoon a girl of fifteen, the daughter of one of the farmers, came to see my husband to complain, with bitter tears, of her unhappy home. Her father, having lost his wife, had married a new one, who was proving the proverbial step-mother. What was the girl to do? Where was she to go? My husband could not see her go without helping her, and it occurred to him at once: Why not give her a chance to study all branches of housekeeping and some branches of farming?

Prize Crop of Sweet Potatoes Raised by Students of the Baron de Hirsch Agricultural School

This was his precedent for opening a girls' department in the Agricultural School. In the teachers' cottage, occupied by the matron and her staff, the upper floor was fitted up for the use of the girls. A course in cooking, general housework, mending and sewing was started, under the direction of our amiable and able matron, the late Mrs. Jennie Steinberg. Work in the hothouse, courses in English, arithmetic and other studies in the schoolroom completed the curriculum of the fifteen girls who were found ready to enter the department. In return for the instruction given them they assisted Mrs. Steinberg in taking care of the dormitories and keeping house for the hundred or more boys.

With the high standards of accomplishment insisted upon by my husband in the school, only those teachers were employed who were able and willing to carry on the work in the right spirit. In answering an applicant for the position of governor, he said:

> It is superfluous for me to state that the position is a very important one, involving a great many moral responsibilities. Only a person who has zeal and enthusiasm for our work need apply. We should like to have a man who loves boys and is a teacher by calling.

It was not, by any means, a light task to control the school and to ensure the contentment of the boys at all times. During the winter months life was easy, as there was no field work; but in summer the boys were particularly apt to be boys. They sought any and every

Interior of Model Greenhouse at the Agricultural School

excuse to "kick." And "kick" they did. One day, I recall, in July, when the matron was unable to work, some trivial item of the meal was missing, and the boys went on a strike. My husband had gone to Philadelphia on business, and learned of the strike only on his return. He was very indignant and wrought up. He trembled with anger and annoyance. Going to the school, he at once called the boys into assembly, and desired to be told their side of the story. It developed that they had no "side" worth presenting. They had no reason whatsoever for complaint. After a talk he informed those who still felt that the substitution of jam for butter, in an emergency, was sufficient reason for their conduct—especially considering the fact that they were receiving free food, clothes, lodging and tuition—that they would be given railroad fares and requested to leave.

A very good idea of the school's activities and standards may be formed from an article on Woodbine which appeared in *Hoard's Dairyman* in 1902. It read:

> The Agricultural School is well housed and equipped with capable teachers, in charge of about one hundred and ten students. The dairy, a credit to any institution, is in charge of Joseph W. Pincus, a Storrs College graduate. A fine dairy it is, with barns and silos. The dairy boys, and indeed most of the agricultural students, are from the city, and in many cases from an orphans' home or from Hester Street, and are sent here to be trained as farmers and as useful, independent men.

The course in dairying starts with stable management. The written examination has, as its first question: "Why a stable?" and then the whys and wherefores of stable management have to be written out in full. When this course is mastered, the milk room education is taken up, a primary course which would be of great advantage to seven out of ten dairymen in the whole country. In a booklet issued by the Woodbine Dairy is told how the animals are kept in clean, ventilated, light stables. A veterinary certificate shows the cows are free from disease. The milking is done by young men of clean habits. The cows' milk, after being weighed, is removed to the milk room and strained, when it is conducted to the cooler. It is there immediately bottled and put into the refrigerator. The milk is analyzed twice a month. Needless to say, all pails, strainers and utensils are thoroughly sterilized.

Mr. Joseph W. Pincus, whose fine bearing and handsome face make him a general favorite with visitors, and seem to fit him for a fashionable drawing room rather than for a farm, took us one day on a tour of inspection of his dairy, which he has made a model for all the country. He pointed out eighteen pedigreed cows with the whimsical remark that he would be at a loss for names for any addition to the herd, as he had already exhausted the names of all his sweethearts!

The school commencements always took place early in the spring, as the graduates and often the under graduates had to leave for positions which were offered them in all parts of the Union. The Agricultural School during the very first years of its experience graduated some of its brightest pupils into agricultural colleges, and found good-paying work for many others who have since become supervisors or foremen on farms, competent florists, poultrymen and heads of large stock farms.

The school semesters were later arranged to be even more elastic for the convenience of the students. A boy spent one whole year at school; then, in the second summer, he was sent out to hold a position in which he would earn both money and experience. In the winter he came back to school again. Thus his stay at the school would be for one summer and three winters—an arrangement particularly well adapted to farm life.

It is difficult to give a systematized account and to show in figures just what the school accomplished for the boys; but my husband always liked to tell of one case that in his estimation, stood out prominently. A boy of about eighteen entered the school. He could speak very little English. All his moral make-up was rather repulsive and to have him near was irritating. He was neither bright in the class-room nor industrious in the field. He did nothing that would warrant our keeping him in the school; but, at the same time, he did nothing that would serve as an excuse for sending him away. So nearly eight months passed without a sign that our school had done anything for him except increase his weight and improve his general health.

But one day he entered the office and told my husband and Dr. Boris Bogen, the principal, that he had learned a little English; that his parents needed his help badly; and that he felt it his duty to go out and work for a

Faculty and Students of the Baron de Hirsch Agricultural School

living and to support them. He said that he appreciated deeply what the school had done for him and added that while he might stay and learn a little more during the winter months, he would be obliged to leave in the summer, just when he might be of some use. He felt that this would be unfair to the school. When he came to take leave we tried to induce him to accept some warm clothing as a little start, until he should secure work, but he declared that the school had done enough for him already, and that he would wear the old clothes in which he came to us.

My husband and Dr. Bogen felt that the boy showed much independence and self-respect. Surely the school had left its good impress on him, but as to his showing on the record, he had done us no credit. So much had been spent on him, with nothing tangible to show on the books; yet few of our graduates could reveal more gratifying results of what we had done for them!

As another and final tribute in relation to the Agricultural School work, I may insert a letter which speaks for itself, coming as it does from a student who had to leave before his course was completed:

My Dear Professor Sabsovich:

You know that I left for the sake of my parents. I tried hard to convince them by letter that I had so much better advantage in the Woodbine Agricultural School, but I did not succeed. Just as a child who leaves his father and mother and brothers and sisters is sorry, so I am sorry. I loved your institution so well for all the good it was doing me and the rest of the boys. I am far away now, but it does not keep me from wishing you and the pupils you direct success and the chance to make out of your institution one that shall be the praise of the Jewish people.

CHAPTER XVI
WOODBINE ENTERTAINS

Woodbine had become a civic entity. It had been developed from a rustic wilderness; first, into a rather formless colony; then into a neat and charming little township. Men unaccustomed to axe and spade had cut down hundreds of acres of trees and laid model roads, which were well-graded and drained, the best roads the county had.

The next necessary step was the building of a commodious country hotel. The only place where visitors could be entertained up to that time was our house. There was not a day that one or more visitors would not come on business to see my husband, often without any previous notice. I would, about 11:30 a.m., receive word from my husband that one, two or even four guests were coming to dinner. "Please be ready for us," would be his message. It was a heavy task in every way, and though after the hotel was built we often entertained at our table, then it was by our own choice.

Very distinguished visitors were thus received. For the little colony among the New Jersey pines had begun to attract national and even international attention. The experiment had ceased to be an experiment and now pointed the way for a much wider application. The numerous visitors were not merely curiosity seekers but men and women of practical vision seeking the man who had blazed trails they were following.

I well remember how, one beautiful morning, when my husband was expecting Gen. Booth-Tucker and Mr. Morris Fels, on the same train with them came Miss Voltairine de Cleyre, a leader of the anarchist group in Philadelphia. My husband and I were quite worried as to how the dinner would proceed in a social way, having at one table a leader of the Salvation Army; a devoted representative of the principles of ethical culture; and a fanatical exponent of free thought, free love and so on. But the splendid way in which my husband turned the conversation into certain channels effectively prevented a single break; not a hitch took place, and for hours we sat after the meal, talking on different topics, the three leaders in their respective movements leaving with the greatest admiration for each other.

The very same year the great Russian writer, Vladimir Korolenko, while on a tour of the United States, visited Woodbine and spent three days with us. He could not admire enough the results that had been accomplished in the colony, and some time after his return to Russia my husband received the following characteristic communication from him, which I translate:

Nijni-Novgorod,
Sept. 10, 1894.

My Dear Woodbine Moses:—

I should not be surprised if in that fine Woodbine town Vladimir Korolenko is being badly scolded; he, who in spite of his promise to write about Woodbine, hasn't even answered your letter. But, if in Woodbine they could know just what happened to Vladimir Korolenko during this time, they would be more lenient with him.

First: Do you remember my story of my little girl, whom I left back in Russia? I then told you how she had held on to my neck and would not let go. I well remember recounting this story one evening, when we were all gathered around your samovar—September 1, according to the Russian calendar—but there was no more Lyolya at that time. I found a telegram upon my arrival in Paris, announcing her death. My wife, who was at the time visiting her brother in Rumania, was unaware of the fact, and I had to take her this sad news. For six long nights and days without a stop I was traveling to Galetz and then to Tulchz. Now, what is there to say? You will easily comprehend my feelings at the time. Upon my return to Russia my two other little girls became ill with diphtheria, one after another in my sister's home; a boy, already in high school, took scarlet fever and died four days later.

These were the conditions that met me upon my return to Russia. Now you see clearly the reason why

I did not write to you. As a matter of fact, I have only just begun to make use of my note-book on America, and have not yet published anything regarding my tour. Every time I have taken up my papers and notes, a sharp pain in my heart would blight every thought and inspiration. So, will you forgive me, my dear Sabsovich? Do you not see how far from the outside world and from letter-writing I was?

Please do write me again about yourself, about the sweetest of little girls, Marusya, and about every one of your family, and do it quickly.

Now that misfortune and heart-pain have left me for a while, I have begun working on the "American Impressions." Possibly I'll start to publish them from October in *Russkoje Bogatstvo*.

First—will be England. Woodbine I will devote one big article to. I'll be very grateful to you if you will send me the very latest news about your life. But the most important thing—after all—will be an assurance that you are not angry with me; that you are enjoying good health; and that you do not forget your (against his will) ungrateful Woodbine visitor.

Meanwhile, I shake your hand heartily.

Your

Vl. Korolenko

I will send you my book within a week or two.

CHAPTER XVII
NEW INSTITUTIONS

To its other glories Woodbine had added also this distinction: It had become a very fine health resort. A young woman, ill from overwork as a teacher in one of the New York schools, visited Woodbine, where she had friends, to recuperate. She returned to the city in splendid health, and in her exuberant gratitude, thus wrote of the place:

> I shall always remember Woodbine with a feeling of pride for our Jewish brothers who seek to eke out a living by earnest and honest labor on the farm and in the several factories. There is so much that is praiseworthy in Woodbine—its plodding and enthusiastic inhabitants, combined with its healthful, lifegiving surroundings, that the three weeks of my stay there can never be effaced from my memory, and as to its effects upon my physical condition, I hope they will be permanent.

This letter and those of many others who happened to spend their vacations in Woodbine brought to my husband the idea of turning one of the farms into a sanatorium, to give city-dwellers suffering from incipient tuberculosis a chance to find new health. A farmer's wife was engaged to take care of the place and attend to the needs of the visitors. It was made a rule that no limit whatsoever must be put on the food. Guests were to have eggs, butter, cheese, milk and vegetables, meat—all they wanted and could consume. Of course the Committee supplied these needs free of charge.

The sanatorium existed for over a year and the results were splendid. With what gratitude did the ailing ones who arrived there pale, with hollow cheeks, leave the place after a stay of five to eight weeks, gaining sometimes from twenty to thirty pounds.

The people of Woodbine began to feel that they were entitled to a synagogue. For years they had worshipped in temporary quarters; but the Woodbine Brotherhood decided now to build its own house of worship. (This was, in itself, a sufficient sign that the colony had become a success!) They subscribed very liberally toward the erection of the building. The Baron de Hirsch Fund loaned them money on the first mortgage; two-thirds of the entire cost in all. The brick used in building was made on one of the farms where the soil was clay, and the structure was amply planned: fifty feet wide and two stories high. The lower one, which was particularly well lighted, was used for years as a school room for the Congregation. Religious instruction was given in the afternoon, kindergarten classes were held there in the morning, and evenings and Saturdays the various clubs and organizations met there. Woodbine was thus ahead of the times in utilizing its public buildings to the full.

We celebrated the dedication of the structure in fine style. Dr. Morris Jastrow officiated. The members of the congregation, in order of seniority, carried the six Scrolls of the Law for the three circuits about the synagogue; the Ark then was opened and the scrolls deposited. The key of the synagogue was presented by a little girl. Herman Rosenfeld, the President of the Brotherhood, a brilliant man of whom any community might have been proud, accepted the key, with a few happy words.

Notwithstanding the inclement weather, the visitors spent a few very pleasant hours visiting the schools, the factories, the sanatorium and other places of interest.

An incident, however, occurred, which might have made the happy occasion end very sadly. We were to entertain at a lunch from fifty to sixty outsiders—guests from New York, Philadelphia and Baltimore—and at supper all the Woodbine settlers. There was a great deal of work to be done and my husband asked me to take charge of the affair. To be assured that some, at least, of my co-workers would be with me from the start, I asked about eight girls to come and stay over night at my home. At 3 a.m. we arose and were greeted by a most unpleasant and unwelcome sound. A heavy rain was pouring floods on the roof and into our windows! Fortunately, true to our previous arrangement, Mr. Schmidt, always ready to help, was at the door with a large covered wagon. We all jumped in and drove to the new building, which was some distance from the house. Leaving the first load of persons and parcels, he returned for another, bringing in addition a half-dozen more volunteer workers. At 4 a.m. the whole staff was ready to begin work, and there was much work to be accomplished by noon.

At 1 p.m. all the tables were set and the whole synagogue beautifully decorated with plants and flowers and bunting. The tables were laden with the finest examples of culinary art that Woodbine housewives could produce—roasted turkeys, chickens, geese and ducks; salads of every description; entrees of every sort; home preserves and canned fruits; jams and marmalades; cakes, strawberry and grape wines.

In another twenty minutes the visitors were expected! It was time to make the coffee! A gasoline stove was brought, and one of the workers turned on the flow of gasoline, but, whether through excitement or inexperience, did not shut it off. At once we were horror-stricken! A great flame shot up to the very ceiling, and an unearthly scream arose of: "Fire; Fire!" With marvelous presence of mind, one of the young girls covered her hair and face with a wet towel, ran forward and turned off the flow of gasoline. But for this action the whole building would have gone up in flames before the visitors had even arrived!

The town had many clubs and benevolent organizations. The Civic Club instructed the people in politics and social literature; a girls' physical culture club had for its object, of course, physical training; a volunteer fire department did efficient work; and a brass band was organized.

The village statutes were so well kept and the law so much respected that a Justice of the Peace was the only officer there, and he was usually busy writing letters in English for the settlers, as he was seldom if ever called upon to exercise his official duties.

The sanitary conditions and other matters relative to the physical welfare of the community were left in control of the Woodbine Improvement Society, organized for this very purpose.

CHAPTER XVIII
THE COLONY INCORPORATES

The matter of taxation and of the control of the schools was the one nearest to the hearts of the people of Woodbine, and it was deemed necessary to face it firmly. My husband knew that Dennis Township was not treating Woodbine fairly in regard to these two important questions. He therefore felt that the Legislature might be induced to grant Woodbine a charter of incorporation on an appeal for justice in these two matters.

We wished to enlarge our schools—as we had over three hundred children at the time—but representatives of the School Board of Dennis Township, the section which would have to share the expense of the buildings and upkeep of the schools, raised an outcry. They would not share the expenses, and the dark forces of Woodbine joined with them. Besides this, my husband showed the Legislature that Woodbine did not have an active voice on the Board of Assessors, and that they were taxed out of proportion to other places in the Township. The legislators were rightly impressed by the petition, and a bill, giving Woodbine a separate political identity, was passed on March 3, 1903.

Mr. Jacob Schiff wrote to my husband, congratulating Woodbine on its new right to self-government.

My husband replied:

> My Dear Mr. Schiff:
>
> I will report your encouraging words at the May meeting that the Woodbine people will hold this week. I hope the responsibility taken by the people of Woodbine will not be too heavy for them and that they will prove themselves worthy of the trust now conferred upon them.

How Woodbine rejoiced when, next morning, the happy news reached it, may be imagined! The first Jewish community to govern itself! Not a whistle blew that day to call the people to work. The schools were closed. The town band and Agricultural School band were out in full force. What a hooraying and tooting and making of music! Where did the youngsters find all the horns and tin trumpets?

The Civic Club hung out a big poster announcing the coming elections of the new borough. There was no question in any mind as to the man to head the list of new officers to be voted for—who should be elected the first Mayor of the first Jewish borough! There was just one name—that of Professor Sabsovich, the father of the place, and, without a dissenting vote, he was elected. Sixteen citizens for the six Councilmen prescribed by law, were nominated. Scarcely a newspaper, large or small, throughout the country, failed to chronicle the event.

First Public Officials of the First Jewish Borough Incorporated in the United States

The real jubilation started at the installation of the newly chosen officers. An inaugural festival of the Borough of Woodbine was entered into by a home commencement of the local public school; music by the Woodbine Military band; recitations by the graduates; tableaux and addresses by the late Dr. Blaustein of New York, the late Dr. Radin and the County Superintendent.

The next day, Memorial Day, 1903, was welcomed by a salute to the flag on the Agricultural School campus, at sunrise. All the one hundred boys of the Agricultural School, in their uniforms, paid the beautiful tribute to the emblem of freedom from the children of foreign lands, who saw not only the natural dawn, but the dawn of a new civic regime. A large banner was presented to my husband—the first Jewish Mayor of the first Jewish community—in the name of the kindergarten. The Girls' Club brought as their offering a wreath of white roses and smilax intertwined, with an emblematic white dove. The day's festivities were varied and interesting, and at twilight there was a pageant, which included members of every organization in Woodbine. This was a sight the like of which Woodbine never saw before, and which would have done honor to any large city. After the parade a ball was given by the fire company. A banquet was given to the newly-elected officers and their wives in the Baron de Hirsch Fund Hall, and thus the celebration of the new borough ended.

Professor Sabsovich had reached the height of his career. He had developed, as one of his admirers has written:

a community where good American citizenship and traditional Judaism go hand in hand. It was Professor Sabsovich's pride to point out to the world how well the Jew performs his duty as a citizen, a patriot and contributor to the well-being of his country when the opportunity is afforded him. It was his great joy to see the farmer and factory-worker, only recently the subjects of oppression and persecution, talk freely, with head erect, of affairs in their new country, state and county, giving their time, money and energy to make their town a model of neatness and cleanliness; to build up an exemplary public school system; to care for the poor and needy; and provide for the moral and physical training of the young generation.

With movements for the public good he was actively concerned throughout all his later years. In this spirit he writes to Rev. Dr. Krauskopf, Philadelphia:

I have read in today's *Public Ledger*, the article "American Citizenship in Russia, the Right Denied," containing your appeal to the Winfield Scott Post, G.A.R. I am deeply touched by your determination to test the rights of an American citizen to brave travel or to reside in Russia, where I know this right will be denied to you. The treaty of 1832 between Russia and the United States gives the right to American citizens to sojourn and reside and secures protection, on condition that they submit to the laws and ordinances prevailing there. You know the laws and ordinances in Russia in regard to the Jews. How can you expect "liberty to sojourn and reside" and protection if the natives are denied these privileges? From the standpoint of international law the Russian government has the right to trample upon your American citizenship, and our government has to permit itself to be snubbed. It is only a logical sequence of the alliance between the Goddess of Liberty and the Demon of Tyranny. Did France fare better than the United States from her shameful and unholy union with Russia? Had she not to stand a snubbing, and very soon after she degraded herself and lowered the dignity of a republic. What other treatment could you expect from a government representing the secret form of autocracy toward the highest form of democratic government on God's earth? Are these two governments naturally not antagonistic to each other? Let the alliance between the United States and Russia cease and the torch of Liberty be lighted as it was under the forefathers and founders of this great democracy! Let all treaties with Russia be abrogated, and the true dignity of this country restored! Let all true American citizens unite in the demand to abrogate the last extradition treaty with Russia! You will do much more for the cause of your brethren in Russia by championing the abrogation movement than by sacrificing your comforts and entering Russia, or trying to enter, in spite of the desire of her government. If countries like the United States, England and France would call back their representatives, they would soon have treaties signed which would secure protection to the citizens of the respective countries as they have in Japan and China.

At the sixth convention of the National Conference of Jewish charities, held in May 1910, he spoke on the subject nearest his heart. Discussing a paper written by Mr. Chester Teller on "Special Education of Jewish Dependent Children," he said:

> I am requested to discuss the excellent paper of Mr. Teller, but I would rather say something about what is to be done with girls and boys between the ages of fourteen and sixteen, not only those dependent on charity, but those who are taken care of by their parents as well.
>
> Children of these ages are too young to enter the skilled professions. The boys usually take unskilled positions in offices, stores, factories and shops, and when they reach the earning wage of sixteen and eighteen, they have small chance of advancing themselves, and having no trade, they drift from one employment to another. If they fail to improve, during this time, the knowledge they have acquired in the public schools, they often forget the little they have learned. This question as to what to do with boys and girls of fourteen to sixteen has become in New York, as elsewhere, a question of vast importance. The City and State of New York are therefore taking steps toward solving the problem by introducing vocational schools. Such a school for boys opened last September for those who have gone to the sixth grade or its equivalent, and they receive not only

academic training, but professional training as well. A considerable part of their time is spent in the shops where printing, carpentry, plumbing, electrical wiring and blacksmithing are taught. Even if this and similar schools should only develop some mechanical attitude in the pupils and reduce the number of drifters, their existence would be justified. The length of the course is from one to three years. The Hebrew Technical School for boys and the Baron de Hirsch Trade School fill partly the demand for trade and technical education for Jewish boys and young men. The Clara de Hirsch Home for working girls and the Hebrew Technical School for girls give industrial training to girls. The Manhattan Trade School for girls was taken over by the Board of Education of the City of New York.

By introducing industrial training as an educational feature in the orphan asylums we should help the movement toward trade education and send out boys and girls with distinctly developed mechanical inclinations and better prepared to take up trade as a life vocation.

As concerns farming, the general impression is that it is no use training our children to take up farming, as farming is not a Jewish occupation and that attempts to make farmers out of Jews have universally proven failures. We have heard a young minister speak on the great possibilities of farming in general in this country, and he proposes, by establishing test farms, to make American farmers out of Jewish immigrants. At the same time he condemned all the previous efforts at colonizing, particularly those in the South and West.

A gentleman from Memphis, also a minister, I believe, tells us of the failure of colonization in Texas. He did not tell us, however, that the immigrants were sent to a fever-stricken district. The fact is, however, that throughout the United States there are thousands of prosperous Jewish farmers. Within twelve miles of Hartford, Conn., for instance, there is a settlement of from twenty-five to thirty prosperous Jewish farmers, who are not only Jews, but good Americans as well. Their houses are equipped with telephone service; some have modern heating appliances, sewerage, and above all—they have modern methods of farming. They are among the best tobacco raisers in the country.

There are also several colonies on the southern part of New Jersey. It is true that the experiences of these pioneers have been of the hardest kind, but they have succeeded in overcoming their difficulties and are now not only very prosperous, but are known as the raisers of the finest sweet-potatoes in the country. They raise the famous "Vineland Sweets."

Although I have had many bitter disappointments in my life's work, I am nevertheless more optimistic than ever as to the future of Jewish farming. With the encouragement that the Jews now have to own and work their own lands, farming is steadily getting a permanent foothold among Jews. In fact, it has long passed the experimental stage, and I hope to see its following grow steadily broader and vaster in numbers; and the orphan asylums would do well to introduce horticulture and agriculture into their educational programs, as there is no doubt that many of the wards would develop an inclination to take up farming as a vocation, and thus many would be afforded a healthy opportunity to grow outside of their congested and overcrowded city employment.

CHAPTER XIX
RECOLLECTIONS

The fulfilment of his life my husband had found in the success of the Woodbine Colony. He turned now to his personal affairs and those of his family, particularly the future of our children. We planned that in 1905 our three daughters were to begin attending high school and college in New York. It was, therefore, necessary to arrange our lives so that we could be with them.

A year previously Mr. Solomons, the general agent for the Fund, had resigned, and the Committee engaged someone to act temporarily, meanwhile looking for a man to take up the work permanently. My husband applied for this position in July 1905, and was promptly accepted. A month later we moved to New York City.

It was responsible work, but without the worries he constantly met with in Woodbine. This was a great relief, for, though his appearance was that of a strong, robust man, he was really of an intensely nervous temperament and serious illnesses had left his heart very weak. He was in touch with Woodbine and its affairs, however, until the very end. Even at a distance he could not be happy without taking an active part in the affairs of the community.

With movements for the public good in New York he was also concerned, and when a hospital in the Bronx was proposed, he stepped in and worked zealously toward making it a success. He was a member of the Board of Trustees and treasurer of its funds. When the dispensary of the hospital was opened, as one of its visiting directors he never missed a Saturday morning there, to assist in one or another capacity.

But all his activities were interrupted when, in February 1914, he fell seriously ill. The best specialists in the city were called and pronounced his case hopeless; but the wonderful care that two physicians, Dr. William Klein and Dr. Paul Kaplan, family friends, gave him day and night, helped him to recover. After two months he was able to leave his bed and go to the country to recuperate. We remained there from April to June, when he decided that he must return to work. We took a bungalow for the summer at the seashore, and four days a week he went back and forth to his work, regardless of the weather. Upon our return to New York we moved to a lower section of the city, so that he might avoid traveling by subway. Here he worked for another year, with his health terribly impaired, and on February 28, 1915, he fell ill, never to be up again.

After his death, his nurse, an elderly woman, told me that she had been at the bedside of many prominent men during her long years of nursing, but never had she taken care of one who, even in delirium—which endured for five days—would speak of men with such kindliness and reveal ideals so high.

Gentle in all his ways, with a heart so great, nature so sweet, and a spirit so lofty, he lies now at rest! May his soul know the peace that in life he always strove for so eagerly!

∾ ∾ ∾

All the circumstances relative to my husband's active life were apparent to the world at large. Everyone who came into contact with him recognized his admirable qualities. I have often seen the practical idealism that made his success possible illustrated in his relations with our children.

Two of our girls—Nellie and Vera, once ran breathless into the house, eyes filled with tears, and voices quivering with sympathy. "Father," they exclaimed, "we have just seen a pitiful sight; there is a poor crippled man walking along the railway track; he looks starved, he is ragged and is begging for some money to enable him to pay his fare to Philadelphia. We ought to help him." "Of course," said my husband, "you should. You have your little banks, why not give the poor man the money?" Both girls quickly emptied their long-time savings and were off.

From the babyhood of Marie on the estate at Yiesk, in Russia, she was a companion of her father. It was a quaint sight to see her toddling after him, wherever he could possibly permit it, about the fields and orchards. A born teacher, he answered all her questions with care and consideration, feeding her mind with what it could assimilate, and incidentally instructing her about the facts of life, as well as about the creatures, the soil and the growing plant life.

A story of that period will show what a small expert the child became, and how expedient her knowledge could prove. The two had gone for a long walk, which, as usual, ended with Marie, tired but triumphant, on her father's shoulders. When he turned to go back, however, my husband, thinking to take a short cut lost his way through the woods and in the similarity of the flat fields. His confidence failed him, but he felt that if he could only strike the borders of the estate he could find his way. Emerging from a clearing in the forest, they came upon another seemingly endless field of grain. He set the child down for a moment and gazed around. Marie put an end to his perplexity:

"Father," she said, embracing the tall stalks. "Our wheat!"

He was surprised and incredulous.

"Our wheat!" she insisted.

And so it was. . . .

When, from Fort Collins, he went to New York City at the invitation of the Baron de Hirsch Fund Committee, she went with him.

Two or three years later, when, after the breach with the farmers at Woodbine, he fell sick and was ordered south to recover, Marie accompanied him as his nurse. Though a mere youngster of eight, she could be fully trusted to take exquisite care of him. In fact, he demurred a little against her exacting caution and the amount of thought which she gave to his health and comfort. He felt that "fussing over him," as he called it, was not the important matter it was made.

Again, when he was staying in the Catskill Mountains after his attack of pneumonia—under her charge, of course—he attempted to neglect her orders. But it was of no avail. Distressed to see him set out on a muddy mountain walk unprotected by overshoes, Marie caught them up and ran after him.

"Put them on," she insisted, "the doctor told me that you mustn't get your feet wet."

Metaphorically speaking, he threw up his hands.

"My dear," he sighed, "I'm glad that you love me, but why be such a *tyrant?*"

Inseparable as they were, however, he would never permit her fervent devotion to concentrate on him or on our family alone. With a deep and selfless wisdom he kept turning her mind outward, directing her budding thoughts and activities toward the service of the community and the broad human interests in which he himself was absorbed.

One winter evening in Woodbine I shall never forget. My husband had been called away to New York, but had promised to return on a certain day, and to bring with him some lovely mechanical dolls for the three children. We were expecting him and the little girls, especially, were looking forward to his coming with eagerness. But when a heavy snowstorm set in, with a driving wind, I hoped he would not try to return. The time for the last express came and passed, and even the children decided that it was better for Papa not to travel on such a night. Just as, however, in spite of their disappointment, they had bravely resigned themselves to retiring, into the room he burst, his arms full of bundles and covered with snow. The gaiety and excitement which followed may be imagined.

"I couldn't wait to see the children's faces when they saw the dolls," he explained, as a plea to me. "I missed the express, but I took the local to the Junction (two miles away) and," he finished, apologetically, "I had to walk the rest of the way."

And though it was by imprudent impulses like these that he was wearing himself out, I could not chide him.

Full of joyous excitement, Vera, our second daughter, a little later exclaimed:

"Papa! is there a happier family than ours, anywhere?"

Truly it seemed that there could not be, and to me no small part of this man's greatness of spirit is reflected in the simple fact that no turmoil of public duties was ever so great as to submerge his devotion to his own or dull his constant effort to make us completely happy.

CHAPTER XX
IN THE HEARTS OF HIS PEOPLE

I visited, last summer, and for the first time in several years, the place of my husband's rest at Woodbine. In the village I had helped him to found, where I had shared every tribulation and triumph of his, I found the memory of him still green and held in fragrant recollection. Many a story I heard for the first time of his friendliness to young and old.

Mrs. N—— related how, when a child of nine, she used to pasture her cow along the railroad tracks. Once the cow broke loose, and trespassed in our flower garden. The gardener, enraged when he saw the cow in his domain, trampling down his floral treasures, ran after her and caught her. Meanwhile the youngster flew breathlessly after her charge; but when she asked him to turn the cow over to her, he said, harshly: "Oh, no. I'll arrest both you and the cow. I'm going to bring you into the Professor's office."

The little girl was terrified as the gardener brought her, with big tears streaming down her face, before my husband. After listening to the tale of the transgression, he turned to the gardener: "You have scared that little child out of her wits. Do you think that all the flowers in Woodbine are worth her tears?" And, telling her gently to be careful next time, he sent her away.

A citizen, the father of several children today, told me that when a student at the Agricultural School, he was walking one moonlight night with two young ladies, and, happening to pass the greenhouse—where he planted the flowers himself—the girls expressed a wish for some, when he gathered a bouquet and gave it to them. But the vigilant gardener was on the watch, and he ran after the party and made a scene, and brought the boy to the office.

After hearing the complaint, my husband asked the gardener whether he had ever been young and walked with a pretty girl in the moonlight? If he had, what would *he* have done? He dismissed the youthful transgressor at once.

Mrs. E. W—— told me that when she was a school-girl of twelve, the road over which the children had daily to travel to school was in very bad condition. It was almost impassable for their bicycles, on which they had not only to transport themselves but their lunch-boxes and books. A group of boys and girls, none of them over twelve, decided to petition the only person they knew they could reach. They came to my husband and explained their difficulties in a most businesslike manner. He gravely listened to their tale, and turning to his stenographer, dictated the following petition, in due form:

> We, the undersigned, wish to put before Dennisville Township our plea to have the road to our school—which is one mile long—put into a condition which will enable us to ride our wheels over it without danger.

He then required each child to sign, and sent the plea to the proper authorities, and during the spring and summer the road was repaired, with others. When school started in the fall, the children came once more in a body to their friend, and thanked him for the part he had taken in obtaining the improved roads. Again he caused them to sign a letter, this time of thanks, and sent it to the town officials who had caused the roads to be repaired.

A woman who began her career as the first kindergarten teacher in Woodbine, told me that her whole attitude towards life had been molded by Professor Sabsovich.

"How we did worship that man!" she said:

> Anything we had done that in any way displeased him was a horrible mortification to us. All he need to have done was to command, and we would have obeyed, but that was not his way. He merely guided, and we followed, feeling safe and happy in doing so.
>
> There was little we could do to express to the Professor our esteem and reverence and the gratitude we felt towards him. On his birthday we usually managed to arrange something that would please him. One birthday, in particular, stands out in my mind.

The boys of the Agricultural School had arranged a little dance, to which only his devoted friends were invited. Just before the day came around, it snowed for three days. Then a thaw set in, followed by a heavy rain. It was an awful night. The slush was so deep that it was hardly possible to pass through it even in boots. We girls were on needles and pins with suspense. We did not dare to venture out, and stood, ready dressed, wondering how we could ever reach the school, which was at some distance from the town proper. The boys had worried, too, but they worried to some purpose! They all managed to get high boots, and went around to our houses, and carried most of the girls over to the school! We were all there, a sight to behold!

Owing to the dreadful storm Professor did not expect any celebration. When he entered the hall and saw the decorations and all of us assembled as though nothing had gone wrong with the elements, he was astounded. His first impulse was to scold us girls for daring to venture out on such a night. But soon his face beamed with pride and gratitude at the thought of such devotion, and the next moment he was happy and gay.

The big constructive work accomplished by the Professor we fully realized in later life. Nevertheless, the real love and devotion with which we always regarded him were founded on a great many of just such instances, which showed the sincere and loving spirit which lighted his every action.

Later in life, when we were scattered in every part of this big country, we always had with us the tender memories of the happy Woodbine days.

Then and now, that occasion which brings any of us together is always hallowed by the beautiful spirit of our beloved teacher and friend, and every one of us feels him or herself a better man or woman because we were privileged to know him.

As I traveled back to New York, I thought how very few men or women have so truly a memorial chamber in the hearts of so many people. The words of George Herbert then arose in my mind, as most fitting and descriptive of the ceaseless unselfish activities of him who we all, with one accord, mourned:

> Only the actions of the just
> Smell sweet and blossom in the dust.

From Those Who Knew
Him Best

The Practical Idealist
By Boris D. Bogen

THE immigration wave from Russia in the eighties included a more or less compact group of young idealists who came not to make a comfortable nest for themselves or to achieve higher standing in their careers, but who dreamt of a better world to live in and dwelt within a Utopia of their own imagining. As a rule, they were wedded to some well-defined theory, and followed the latter with the fervor of fanaticism. In the course of their early experiences in America they encountered many a stumbling block in the way of the realization of their dreams and were, as time went on, shifted to other and more prosaic pursuits.

There were only a few who remained bound to their ideals and although the workaday world found them thrown upon their own resources, they gathered together on the mutual ground of idealism. Their gathering place would be one of the tea houses on the East Side, where the bearers of "welt schmertz" nightly wended their way, discussed over and over again their complex problems, quarreled over purpose, solution and method, and talked and talked and talked. Among these young dreamers were men of high intellect and strength of reasoning power. One bore a different expression from his fellows—a purposeful, steady and firm resolve. He was not living in New York, but he frequently visited the city and then he too would join the "Russian Colony."

At the tea house he was one of them and his visits were hailed as an event. He was welcomed royally. He would listen to the endless discussions and inquire into the details of the various local developments. But he never failed to impress upon his subject-matter his own personality. Idealist as he was, he did not detach himself from the world of practical things. He too had an idea of a universal and all-inclusive social order, but he did not insist upon the necessity of applying this world program within a limited sphere. All the world was his, so far as his sympathies were concerned, but what interested him was the actual contribution that he and his fellows could make.

To these fellows of his he turned with his appraisal. What can you expect of people who fritter their lives away in useless discussion? You neglect your bodies—what use can you be to the world if you cannot look after yourselves? Why do you stay in the city? What future does this cafe hold in store for you? Bent on destroying the lure of the city, he never tired in picturing the beauties and glories of the country. He loved nature; the city, he felt, was not the place for mankind to grow.

He suffered in his realization that the life of his comrades was based upon a wrong tendency—a tendency that seemed to grip all about him. He knew that so long as they clung to the city, there could be no hope for his people. For it was the fate of the Jews that lay nearest his heart. In America he saw a wonderful opportunity for Israel to start life anew. But this could not be brought about by a passive attitude on the part of the leaders among the Jews; it was they who must blaze the path. The problem was not one for theorizing—the active energies of many leaders would be needed—to bring the Jew into the country where he might find himself.

He did not limit his propaganda to his intimate circle of friends—he tried to exemplify his program within himself. For years before coming to America he had devoted himself to preparation for his life's work. He came to the New World a full-fledged trained agriculturist, ready and eager for the task he had set for himself.

The idea of settling the newcomers on the soil was in vogue in those days. The Baron de Hirsch Fund had undertaken to finance various activities with this end in view. And for the leader in this gigantic task they selected this dreamer, who came to the barren stretches of Woodbine and claimed it for his promised land.

Thus it was that Professor Sabsovich entered upon his life work. The location for the experiment had, unfortunately, been selected before his appointment. But, in the face of numerous and tantalizing difficulties, he plunged into his task.

First, it was merely a question of placing a limited number of independent farmers in that region, thus forming the nucleus of a Jewish agricultural colony. But as the work grew new problems presented themselves, each leading up to another and forcing a constant expansion in the activities. How could the products be marketed? How could the lure of the city be counteracted? Questions such as these never ceased to present new opportunities for service.

The man in charge soon became the soul of the entire movement. He saw the problem as something more than a farm-letting venture. He lived in the village. He fought stubborn opposition. He stimulated the people who controlled the funds to see greater visions of what they might do. He aroused the interest and enthusiasm of the people for whom he worked. Leaping beyond the boundaries of his set program, he devised new plans and, throwing the whole force of his being into the struggle, brought about great pieces of social construction almost single handed.

The first year of the twentieth century saw Woodbine as a neat little town sheltering over a thousand souls, boasting of the best schools in the county, streets, water works, electric power, a synagogue, stores and four or five factories. But this was not all.

A special Agricultural School, started with practically nothing, was now a reality. In the beginning it had been a simple step. Just a few farmers' sons, receiving instruction from the father of the enterprise, spent thrilling evening hours and the precious free hours of the day with him. The instruction returned them to the farm, skilled and equipped. The inspiration led them on, through college and into the world of success. So the idea of the school took root and started to grow.

Modest surely—just for the children of the farmers—only a small investment. But before a year or two had passed the school had taken its place as a new center of educational experimentation. Buildings came up. A faculty was established. The Paris Exposition awarded the Woodbine Agricultural School the Grand Prix in 1900, and in 1902 this triumph was crowned by the Gold Medal at the Buffalo Exposition.

So Professor Sabsovich toiled on and dreamt on. Jewish farmers were settled on the lands and encouraged to go on. Industries were attracted to the village, so that they might draw the Ghetto dwellers from the city streets. The school, typifying the new ideal for Jewry, stood as a beacon, lighting the way. But Sabsovich did not stop here.

He developed a plan by which the real merit of the Jew as a citizen might be demonstrated. It was just at this time that public opinion was stirred against the immigrant by accusations that he was degrading American politics. The corruption brought about by political rings was blamed upon the Jewish newcomer. It is not true, Professor Sabsovich claimed, that the Jew betrays his privileges. Whatever weakness he may show is due to his surroundings, to influences working in spite of him and against him. Give him a chance to participate in his government, explain to him, in terms that he can understand, his high privileges and responsibilities. Then will the Jew serve as a model of good citizenship. Here again a practical demonstration was needed to prove the claim.

At once he gave himself to this new idea. A separate borough charter was obtained for Woodbine; it became a political unit conducted solely by Jews. It showed splendid signs of wholesome communal development. Citizenship was no more a perfunctory obligation. It became rooted in the very lives of the inhabitants of the little village. A city hall was established; a civic club sprang into being and flourished; a modern health movement was launched; a systematic educational regime was established. The school system in Woodbine today is still the best in the County.

So Woodbine grew. Here the Jews, left to themselves, developed a sound social body, busying themselves with agriculture, industry and trade. Here, close to nature, their children flourished safe from the negative forces of the city streets. Here every home was a temple and the temple was the heart of the community.

Twenty-five years of pioneer work bore fruit. The soil, once barren of everything but scrub bushes and white sand, had been transferred into a beautiful town with hundreds of homes, the thriving bustling activities of a tiny city and, on the outskirts the busy farms, the beginning and the sole idea upon which the entire enterprise was started.

But these physical things cannot tell the story of Professor Sabsovich's entire achievements. His greatest contribution, perhaps, was his influence as a leader in the lives of the people. Hundreds, nay thousands, of young men were inspired by him to follow higher ideals, to prepare themselves for service, to consecrate themselves for a cause. Entire families and their children's children, learned through him to love nature and the country life.

Later he assumed the duties of General Manager of the Baron de Hirsch Fund in New York where, devoting all that was in him to the development of the Fund activities, he found time and opportunity to extend his influence into the various fields of Jewish social service, in the days when this service was just beginning to develop into a definite professional field.

When Professor H. L. Sabsovich died, he left to all Jewry a legacy that grows greater with each passing year. To the Jewish social workers his life holds a meaning especially dear. His devotion to the cause, his persistence and faith in the possibility of getting things done, in spite of opposition and indifference, his courage to experiment on propositions that were likely to prove failures and, above all, his absolute identity with the work he did. He lights the pathway of the social worker as a living inspiration, and his work points out the way as a guide in what the future must bring.

A Pioneer Social Worker
By Solomon Lowenstein

To be most authentic, an account of Professor Sabsovich as a social worker should be written by one who knew him intimately during the time of his great work in the building up of the Woodbine Colony, but unfortunately most of his colleagues of that period are no longer available in social work. This defect, however, is rendered less serious by the beautiful and simple presentation of his activities at that time contained in the foregoing memorial by Mrs. Sabsovich.

To those of us who were associated with him in his social service in later years, the impression that remains is chiefly one of a thoroughly human, sympathetic personality whose really positive force and firm decision were always clothed by a congenial and lovable personality. His was a mind whose honesty no one could doubt for an instant—it was crystal clear. The elements of any question, no matter how complicated or intricate, revealed themselves to him almost instantly and he was able to formulate the resulting proposition in a form so clear and simple as to be intelligible to any who cared to listen. He knew no discrimination because of position, reputation, or wealth. He was fearless in his judgment, once convinced of the rectitude of his position, no matter what institutions or personalities were involved. He had a power of righteous indignation, at times seemingly inconsistent with his ordinary gentleness of manner whenever he believed that injustice was being done, especially to the weak or the subordinate.

His work was carried on at a time when the trained social worker was still occupying a new and indefinite position among his professional brethren, when ethical standards had not yet been developed and when the relations between paid workers and their volunteer boards of trustees were not always either harmonious or dignified.

Though his own position was a happy one as a result of years of acquaintance and common work, he felt most keenly the difficulties of some of his less fortunate colleagues and was foremost among those striving to dignify the position of social worker and to improve the personnel of those engaged in these important tasks. As a result he was among the first to urge the need and to co-operate in the creation of special courses and schools for Jewish social workers and was particularly interested in the establishment of a plan for retirement allowances and pensions for Jewish social workers so that the work might at least offer financial security and attractiveness equivalent to that in the field of education. As President of the Jewish Social Workers of Greater New York and as Chairman of a special committee for this purpose appointed by the National Conference of Jewish Social

Work, he labored to the full extent of his strength for this desired end.

He was one of a small group of executives in New York, most of whom have now been lost to the profession, by death or retirement, who for a number of years met monthly at the homes of the members for the discussion of questions of common interest and for the improvement of their own work, that of the organizations which they represented and of Jewish social service in general. It is impossible to estimate the value of these meetings in the progress of Jewish social service in New York and particularly in the development of professional spirit among those privileged to be of the group. Among all the members there was none whose advice was so eagerly sought or whose judgment more respected than Professor Sabsovich. In this connection he displayed another of the charming qualities which so endeared him to his friends—the delightful hospitality of his home when in the regular course the group had the happiness to be the guests of Professor and Mrs. Sabsovich. His entertainment was so generous yet so thoroughly informal and congenial, there was such a pervasive hospitality that the meetings at his home were likely to endure far beyond the normal hour.

To the rest of the group, chiefly Americans by birth and early training, it was a rare advantage to be able to absorb from Professor Sabsovich (in this respect the late Dr. Blaustein should also be mentioned) the spirituality and idealism represented and acquired by them from their early life in Russia. Their wholehearted devotion to the masses of their people, the revolutionary ideals that they brought with them and the humanity of the relationship, which they typified, gave to us of a different background an inspiration and a stimulus the value of which cannot be overestimated.

Thus in simplicity, in earnestness and enthusiasm he worked himself away. He was so quiet, so gentle in his zeal that we did not realize the extent to which he was giving of his strength to his daily work. The end came too soon and unawares. We were left with a sense of profound loss. We had lost a true friend and a noble man but the inspiration of his influence and his character has served to hearten many a worker who had the blessing of his friendship and shared with him in common service for the Jewish people.

A Life Nobly Lived
By Bernard A. Palitz

PROFESSOR H. L. SABSOVICH stands in a niche all his own in the field of Jewish social service. His life was whole-heartedly, honestly and unselfishly dedicated to the hope of creating a new era in the history of his suffering people. In his labor for their welfare there was a spirituality that fired him with noble ambition, caused him to understand and feel the actual needs of the Jewish race as a whole and developed in him to a high degree that power of concentration, that tireless zeal and unshadowed depth of faith in the possibilities of a new Israel in this new land which made him notable from the day he shook the dust of his native country from his feet.

His personality will for a long time, like a stream of light, linger in the memory of a host of friends and followers. As an exponent of the highest type of social workers, his name will forever be associated with the most interesting page in the history of Jewish social service in America. His life has this double interest for this as well as the generations to come.

Professor Sabsovich came to his new land with his work found and mapped out and consecrated to the service of a cause, the underlying purpose of which was to tear out by the root the foe's repeated declaration—made in ignorance and based on twisted historical facts—that the Jew is inherently averse to productive labor, and to bring real and permanent blessedness and peace to the Jewish immigrant running from the hosts of maddened mobs and oppressive, degrading, lawless laws.

Jews were permitted, against the wishes of Peter Stuyvesant, by the Dutch West India Company to settle in New York, on condition "that the poor among them shall not become a burden to the community but be supported by their own nation." Little did they suspect that the time was coming when the Jewish settlers were not alone being prevented from falling a burden, but, by attaching themselves to the soil, were gradually lining up as providers for the community, interested, as loyal citizens and responsible owners of homes, in its permanent welfare, morally and materially.

To bring about this improvement on the stipulation of the Dutch West India Company was the ultimate aim of Baron de Hirsch, the ardent desire of the administrators of his foundation, and the unremitting efforts of their conscientious resourceful collaborator, Professor Sabsovich.

Professor Sabsovich dealt with ideas which he strove, with sincere desire and proper understanding, to bring into real life. Contemplating on the past and present of his weary race, and through his close and intimate study of the relations of the non-Jewish to the Jewish masses, he became aware that the political and social emancipation of the Jew, in any land, is not and will not, by itself, solve the Jewish problem and that our pointing with pride to Jewish great lights who won fame and stand high in the world's larger affairs does not affect the state of mind of the neighboring masses who come in contact, in their everyday life, with the Jewish masses only. He was convinced through personal observations and reflection on the incessant trials of the Jew, whether in enlightened or unprogressive lands—trials differing only in color and in form but not in substance—that hand in hand with the spiritual and intellectual reform there must come the economic emancipation of the Jewish masses which will make them an indispensable factor of their country's material existence and a part of the nation's nursing force.

Recognized as a true social worker, equipped, in soul and mind, with the proper strength to cope with big problems, he was placed in charge of one of the most important tasks of the Baron de Hirsch Fund—that of directing the agricultural movement among the Jewish immigrant population.

Activities in this direction were started in this country long before his advent, but the movement was all in a fog. The early attempts at colonization and farm settlement and things accomplished are too well known to need reiteration here. The same characteristic marks noticeable in individual ventures made in haste, without due consideration and patient study, are found in philanthropic enterprises, with emotion as the chief moving factor and not based on studied and thoroughly analyzed experience and not directed by a trained scientific mind.

As one looking for results rather than aiming to simply "do things" he was determined to work out the agricultural activities among Jews to their proper consequences. While the aim of the movement was mainly economic, the means to reach it, he held, must run along both educational and physical lines. Being himself highly intellectual and knowing that in order to fit one for leading positions in the great agricultural industry in this country, he must be given an opportunity to acquire a thorough practical as well as theoretical training, Professor Sabsovich sought to interest the young rather than the adults.

"Not only," said he, "is it necessary to change the physical habits and customs of the prospective farmer but a mental turn-over must be affected in order to bring results."

The general absence of any vision on the part of many leaders in American Israel, regarding the agricultural movement, was a source of grave concern to him. So far the activities had been confined to settling on farms men of mature age with habits of living formed and city ideas of life embedded in them for centuries.

Considering this movement for the future rather than for the immediate present, he addressed himself to the young and still growing minds and out of his efforts, the Baron de Hirsch Agricultural School for the Jewish youth became a reality.

In his annual report for the year 1896, Professor Sabsovich writes:

> Jewish agriculture in whatever part of the globe it may be practiced, has a special interest and is of a particular importance, not common to agriculture as such, and namely, it is a living proof of the falsehood of the assertion of the political anti-Semites in Russia, that the Russian Jew avoids productive work, especially the noble vocation of the tiller of the soil. It further proves that whenever and wherever the Russian Jew enjoys political freedom and freedom of selection of a calling, he does not neglect agriculture as well.
>
> Anything which helps to develop Jewish agriculture is of great importance above named. Our school which has grown from a very modest beginning is becoming one of the factors of improving and enlarging of Jewish agriculture in this country. That there is a tendency on the part of a large portion of newcomers to our country among the Russian Jews to devote their means and abilities to agriculture, the past has proved to be so.

Agricultural training for the young was at the same time calculated to serve as a medium for the betterment of the material condition of the existing and prospective farmers of the older generation who, lacking the practical and theoretical knowledge of American farming, needed guidance and advice. In the same report Professor Sabsovich writes:

It was natural to provide an institution for disseminating agricultural knowledge among the Jewish farmers by giving agricultural education to their children, and by preparing agricultural instructors and inspectors.

The early stages of the career of the Agricultural School were not without disappointments and hardships. At best it was a journey of some swerves and concussions. But devotion and persistency—his outstanding characteristics—increased with the growth of his conviction that the "out of the city and back to the country" idea was taking root in the heart and mind of the tired wanderer himself. No obstacle or hardship ever discouraged him or deterred him from prosecuting his task. For though an idealist, his actions were not founded on imagination nor grounded on fancifulness, but always carried the stamp of a constructive and creative mind.

The enthusiasm with which hundreds of Jewish young men have entered and passed the Agricultural School, and adjusted themselves permanently to the farming trade and country life after graduation; the fact that shortly after the opening of the school in Woodbine a need for another similar institution became apparent, resulting in the establishment of the National Farm School; the rapid spread of Jewish farming settlements in every State of the Union, the material betterment and general improvement of which is due, in a large measure, to the valuable educational help given by the graduates of the two schools; and finally, the increasing number of Jewish students attending State agricultural institutions in the country, secondary schools and colleges, bring to light ample proof of the correctness of his judgment and his correct appraisal of the requirements and possibilities of Jewish agriculture.

It also completely disproves the erroneous conclusion of our foes and friends alike that the Jew is too good a tradesman to make a good agriculturist. What is true is the fact that the Jew is too vigorous intellectually and has amassed during his long centuries of exile too large a fund of mental energy to limit himself to work of a physical character only. Agricultural education for the Jewish youth combining mental action and physical equation was the movement shouldered by Professor Sabsovich, encouraged by the Trustees of the Baron de Hirsch Fund. In this he saw the salvation of his people; through this he comprehended a Judaism come back to its own and by this he sought to silence its traducers and libelers.

Will this product of a useful life continue to blossom and bear further and larger fruit so that in due time a good part of our people will live in peace that only nature can provide? Will our practical leaders see the danger that threatens our moral, physical and political status and bend their energies towards the creation of a new social posture for our people so well started by our deceased friend? Will our philanthropists analyze and learn from the past and find out how much calumny there would have been checked, how much suffering prevented and how many lives spared if the bulk of our people had been tillers of the soil instead of children of the Ghetto? Will those who have minds and hearts also have the vision to see that the changing order requires more preventive than remedial charity! Will our statesmen remember the cruel and unceremonious answer given by the Polish Premier to a Jewish delegation that he and the Polish people would rather see the Jews leave that country and, this being manifested covertly or openly by many other governments and peoples, will not those who watch over the destinies of the people see that no group or part of a population, attached to land as an essential limb of the national body, can be easily uprooted, heartlessly persecuted and suffered to be tossed about from place to place? Will they not all make haste and avail themselves of the golden opportunity offered by this free land, with its millions of inviting acres, and with the art of agriculture making giant strides, and thereby save millions of our brethren from torture and degradation in the future, which has not or rather could not be done in the past?

Let us hope, yes. Professor Sabsovich blazed the way!

Next to his intensive study and sublime efforts in the interest of agricultural education for the Jewish youth and the promotion of the farming industry among the Jewish population in general, his main and most important work, from the point of view of community organization and methods of Americanization, was the founding and up-building of the town of Woodbine, which formed another chapter of a life replete with service and unselfish labor.

Here, as in the many other activities of the Baron de Hirsch Fund, his native power, executive ability, genuine devotion and self-denial have manifested themselves in their full strength, and here, his personality, his character and his wonderful gift of inspiring people with confidence in themselves and loyalty to the cause he represented, found scope and outlet.

When it became evident that Woodbine could not permanently exist as an exclusively agricultural settlement and that, in order to insure its economic stability, it must be reinforced by industrial opportunities, the Trustees of the Fund found Professor Sabsovich ready for the gigantic task of building the community physically, educationally, socially and politically.

It is well to remark here, that, although the Baron de Hirsch Fund was the sponsor of Woodbine and stood behind all its initial undertakings, it was the early settlers themselves who, by hard labor and with the tenacity and endurance of the pioneer, have wholeheartedly cooperated in the working out of the problem of their new social unit, and who have proved themselves able to meet the requirements of American life and American concepts.

In Professor Sabsovich they found their inspiration and his keen and practical insight into human nature and human motives enabled him to awaken the dormant qualities in men who, as free individuals and eager to tie themselves permanently to their new home-land, soon evinced their own vitality and discovered in their leader a personality with whom they could readily come to a feeling of unrestrained intimacy.

The founding of the town of Woodbine and the decision of the Trustees of the Fund to stimulate its growth and development constituted a duty of the hour. It was along the lines of a general course of action necessitated by the conditions that faced American Jewry, when the proportion of immigrants settling in the crowded cities threatened to produce a frame of mind in the American people against unrestricted immigration.

Various plans have then been devised to help divert the stream from the large centers along the Atlantic coast to the interior of the country and smaller communities. The Baron de Hirsch Fund sought to avoid serious consequences by helping other organizations to establish immigrants in less congested localities, by supporting farm settlements, by erecting dwellings near New York, known as Borough Homes, and by subsidizing industries in Woodbine.

Professor Sabsovich paid particular attention and took special pride in Woodbine not alone because of the advantages of country life and wholesome social surroundings it offered to the immigrant, but also because of the monumental opportunity it afforded to demonstrate before the world the willingness and readiness of the Jew to adapt himself to the new forces which are moving a free people and his recognition and acceptance of the duties and responsibilities imposed, as well as the rights and privileges bestowed upon him by a free democracy.

Indeed, the early Woodbine settlers have proven that the real and immediate solution of the problem of Americanization lies not so much in organized propaganda and neighborhood influence as in the mental makeup and ethical conception of the immigrant himself.

Without any external and, if I may so call it, professional Americanization programs, not brought in direct and frequent contact with the native population, the newcomers at Woodbine have, spontaneously and instinctively, as if by the mere breath of the free atmosphere, taken America as their ideal and reality. And it cannot be otherwise. Those who know the Jewish life in the centuries of wandering and the source from which it draws its spiritual and cultural subsistence must know the Jewish view and interpretation of the relationship of the individual to the interests of his nation and the social structure as a whole. In the words of Dr. Kohler:

> The Jewish love of learning led to an ever greater longing for truth by adding wisdom of other cultured nations to its store of knowledge.[1]
>
> The idea of interdependence and reciprocal duty among all members of the human family forms the outstanding characteristic of Jewish ethics.[2]
>
> In fact, the State which guarantees to all its citizens safety, order and opportunity under the law and which arranges the relations of the various groups and classes of society that they may advance one another and thus promote the welfare and progress of all, is human

1 *Jewish Theology*, by Dr. K. Kohler, p. 358.
2 *Ibid.*, p. 319.

society in miniature. Here the citizen first learns obedience to the law which is binding upon all alike, then respect and reverence for the authority embodied in the guardians of the law who administer justice "which is God's" and hence also loyalty and devotion to the whole, together with reciprocal obligation and helpfulness among separate members and classes of society.[3]

The Jewish immigrants in Woodbine started the building of American public schools for their children and organized themselves into political groups and civic associations, in order to understand better how to serve their new land, in the same spirit and with the same enthusiasm, as they erected their synagogues, formed brotherhoods and other religious and charitable institutions. Professor Sabsovich understood and encouraged them in their social and civic aspirations, as in their economic and educational strivings and, as leader, friend and counselor, grew in love and esteem of every man, woman and child in town.

His care and solicitude for the good name of the newly formed community knew no bounds and he was as elated over the little boy or girl winning the prize in the intercountry spelling contest as he was proud of one of the graduates of the Baron de Hirsch Agricultural School becoming the head of the Agricultural Department of the State and an authority on soil bacteriology.

As early as 1892 he reports thus to the Trustees of the Fund:

3 *Ibid.* p. 320.

How great such progress has been is best shown by the present aspect and condition of Woodbine; its streets, roads, dwellings, schools, hotel, electrical plant, industrial establishments and farms, are more eloquent than any description that might be written. All those who saw Woodbine eighteen months ago when it was nothing but a great barren plain, covered with a growth of stunted bushes, must acknowledge without reserve that a laudable and well-directed energy, supplemented by the efforts of new immigrants has here opened up a broad field of prosperity. Hither we invite the narrow-minded enemies of our immigrants to convert them in the face of such achievements, into friends.

Again, in his report for the year 1898, he writes:

The peaceful and progressive activity of the Woodbine population is conquering the prejudices of our neighbors and there is hardly a thinking man in Cape May County who is not fast becoming convinced that Woodbine has come to stay, not only for the benefit of its own population, but also for the community at large. The intelligent elements of the County, as represented in the County Teachers' Association, the Association of Members of the several Boards of Education, and the leading farmers, on several occasions, at their Annual Meetings and Institutes have expressed their appreciation of the educational work carried on by us; in fact, our Agricultural School is becoming so popular that the Farmer's Institute of the Cape May County

Board of Agriculture, under the auspices of the State Board of Agriculture and the State Grange was held at De Hirsch Hall, which is also selected as the place for the next Annual Meeting of the Association of the Educational Boards of the County.

That not only the County but also the State authorities recognized the value of his work in Woodbine and his personal merits has been shown by the honor conferred upon him in electing him a life member of the Board of the State Agricultural College, in 1905.

His relations to the people of Woodbine were fatherly and marked with most unselfish generosity. He was entirely free from all personal bitterness. On one occasion the writer was handed by him a letter addressed to him by a disgruntled manufacturer. The letter was full of insults and vilifications. To the questions what he will do about it, he answered, in his characteristic way, that his personal feeling did not matter, as long as the writer of the letter was otherwise a beneficial factor in the town.

As could be expected under the circumstances, Woodbine, as a typical Jewish immigrant community, has focused the attention of many a sociologist interested in the life and doings of former abject subjects of dark countries and now sovereign citizens of this truly blessed Commonwealth. Among the many visitors and students of sociology there were some who justly or unjustly found fault with the management or the people. Professor Sabsovich never failed to explain honest criticism and to challenge censures called out by ulterior motives, or false observation.

It may not be amiss at this juncture to correct a statement made by Mr. Peter A. Speek in his otherwise attractive treatise on the absorbing question of Americanization. In his book, *A Stake in the Land*, page 176, there appears the following passage:

> The local manager of the Hirsch fund in Woodbine, New Jersey, a Jewish colony, stated that there is in the colony a Hebrew school supported by individuals and to a certain degree by the Hirsch fund. It is a Hebrew school connected with activities of the synagogue, maintained for religious purposes. It corresponds to the parochial school of Christian Churches. About sixty pupils attend this school.

This is entirely contrary to the facts. The Hebrew school referred to is not a parochial school. It is a school where Hebrew is taught. It is a place where the children are given religious instruction, after the regular public school hours. There was no such thing with the Jewish people of Woodbine as a parochial school, in the sense and with the purpose it is maintained and conducted by other denominations mentioned in other parts of his book and justly criticized by him. There was not and there is not one child of school age in Woodbine who does not attend the public schools and the great majority of the graduates of the latter enter high schools. These schools are maintained partly by the State and partly by the Borough and supervised by the County Superintendent, and their curriculum is fixed by the State and County authorities. There is not a young man or a young woman in Woodbine whose tongue is not English and whose thought is not American. They are, of course, taught by their parents the tenets of their religion. It would indeed be a sorry departure if this were not the case.

On the other hand, a more thorough observer, who also visited Woodbine recently for the same purpose, has the following to say about the educational activities of the Jews of that town:

> While the center of the Bohemian community was seen to be the freethinking society, and that of the Dutch community the church, in the case of this Jewish community the center is the public school. A supervising principal is in general administrative charge. The present incumbent has held this position some twelve years. Although himself a Christian, he is thoroughly interested in and identified with the community, as are the members of his family.
>
> School attendance is excellent, and there is little absence, except on the part of non-Jewish children, in whose case regulations are not strictly enforced. There are a few children of the local Native American stock, who are unprogressive and deficient both physically and mentally. Only about 10 percent of the Jewish children leave to go to work before completing the eighth grade. Of those who remain, close to 90 percent go to high

school; and of these, in turn, nearly half finish the high school course.[4]

From the start the influence of Professor Sabsovich permeated every phase of the town development and especially education matters. But he was careful not to interfere with the desire of the people and their freedom of action, and it was one of the remarkable traits of his character that he knew how to fix the boundaries of his influence.

When Woodbine was incorporated into a separate Borough he felt that his mission as leader of the community had ended, and that the people would achieve more in the absence of outside influences than in their presence, when they themselves are the sole keepers of the doors of opportunity. Actuated by this motive, he accepted the post of General Agent of the Baron de Hirsch Fund, when it was offered to him, in 1905.

His coming from Woodbine to New York was not to Professor Sabsovich a sudden move from the desert to a cultivated field. For though in Woodbine, he was active in a distinct sphere of social endeavor, his interest in general charity and philanthropic affairs of the Jews in America was ever alive and he was always a conspicuous figure in the deliberations of the Jewish Social Workers at their national conferences. The monograph on the way Jewish charity was dispensed in Russia, submitted at one of these conferences, by him and Dr. David Blaustein, was an important contribution to Jewish charity liter-

4 *America via the Neighborhood*, pp. 50–51, by John Daniels.

ature, and his views on general human activity were sought and respected at those gatherings.

Though his duties as General Agent of the Baron de Hirsch Fund were numerous, he was ever ready to give his time and lend his counsel to other great questions pertaining to the welfare of the Jews.

He took a prominent part in the formation of the Jewish Immigration Committee and the National Jewish Immigration Council, whose purposes were to see that the immigrant upon his arrival receives proper treatment and to coordinate immigration societies in the several ports of entry, and served as secretary of the former organization from its inception, in 1910, to his death.

For some time he was President of the Society of Jewish Social Workers of Greater New York. In this capacity he learned and formed his opinion on the general status of the Jewish social worker in this country, materially and in other respects. The various opportunities offered in social work have been analyzed and individualized by him for the benefit of the younger workers, and the bringing about of a new standard in the profession was one of the many problems in which he was concerned during the last years of his earthly life.

He strongly advocated the opening of special courses for the training of Jewish social workers, and the idea of founding a social workers' pension fund originated with him and was given expression at the National Conferences. In his memorable address, delivered before the National Conference in June 1911, he made the following striking remarks:

Jewish philanthropic and charitable institutions in the United States are no longer satisfied with the services of the amateur worker or of the down and out members of respectable families of the communities. They want well-prepared and thoroughly qualified workers.

There is at present a scarcity of well-prepared and qualified workers. Last year about half a dozen fine positions in the country went a-begging.

To attract the Jewish young men and young women and to retain them in service, the following are important requisites:

1. To raise social service to the dignity of a profession by demanding professional preparation on the part of the social worker.

2. To offer to the prospective social worker a salary sufficient for a modest but decent living.

3. To assure the social worker that he or she will not starve in the case of a breakdown or a total disability, and that his or her family will not suffer should they die.

In the history of Jewish social service the work of Professor Sabsovich will be recorded and judged by the fruit it has borne, and by the unselfish motive with which this work was carried on. For he did not make his profession "a crown wherewith to aggrandize himself," nor "a vestibule that he may enter a palace" of ease and riches. The field of social effort for the good of his people was his palace and the burdens he carried all through life were his crown.

He loved his burdens and bore them gladly, patiently and willingly. Like Hamsun's Isak, "life without a load was" to him "no life at all."

Our Teacher
By Saul Drucker

"A good name is rather to be chosen than great riches, and loving kindness, rather than silver and gold."

And because he had chosen as he did, his mourners, whose names are legion, will cherish the good name he left and keep the heritage of loving-kindness he gave them, with greater pride than if it had been silver and gold bequeathed.

Born in Russia, that most unfortunate of all birth-places for the Jew, Hirsch Loeb Sabsovich in the early adolescence of his manhood, while still a student at the University, keenly realized the efforts made by the anti-Semitic government to dwarf the Jew both physically and mentally, and cripple his opportunities. He knew the futility of appealing to the justice of officials who excused their mediæval persecutions and cruelties under the plea that the Jew is a consumer and not a producer; he knew, too, the several spasmodic and theatrical attempts made by the government to make the Jew a producer of the soil, which had suffered disastrous failure, naturally enough, because the Jew had neither the knowledge nor the wherewithal to become a soil producer. It was then that the conviction took firm root in his mind that nothing like being a producer of the soil would bring independence and happiness to his people, and gradually the "Back to the Soil" Movement originated in his brilliant brain.

He immigrated to the United States, and at once interested himself in Jewish colonization. Within three years of his landing in this country, his views on the subject attracted such favorable attention that, while still occupying the position of professor of chemistry at the Colorado State Agricultural College, he was invited by the trustees of the Baron de Hirsch Fund to take charge of the Woodbine Colony. The task confronting him was an extremely difficult one. His object was to teach scientific farming to the few who really, by the sweat of their brows, eked out a wretched subsistence from the soil, and to interest those who accepted the new idea with the presumption that it would be easy to resume an avocation which centuries upon centuries ago had been wrested from their fathers. But the chopping down of trees, the selling of wood by the cord, the digging out of stumps, and the general labor of tilling the soil were not found to be adaptable to the first settlers, and particularly not to the younger generation of would-be farmers. A problem presented itself, then, the very problem that today confronts the non-Jewish farmer: "How is the younger generation to be kept on the farm?" With the Jews, however, the problem was more serious, since the agricultural life of the people depended upon interesting the youth in the soil.

It was then that Professor Sabsovich proved himself to be a good psychologist. In his thirst for knowledge and opportunity the young immigrant would not be satisfied with mere farm labor, no matter how promising was the prospect as a future tiller of the soil. As a result of this observation the Agricultural School of Woodbine was established, where the children of farmers, and others attracted by agriculture, could be given a general education while learning scientific farming. It was an experiment, but so well was a demand fulfilled, and such was its progress, that it became an established institution, thanks to the indefatigable labor, patience and energy of the man whose fertile mind conceived it.

The colony and the school prospered, one gaining strength from the other, and both mutually helpful. The school attracted attention throughout the country, the trustees of the Baron de Hirsch Fund were interested and enthusiastic, and the Professor realized his dream of educating the youth of his people for the soil, so that the Jew should take naturally and willingly to agriculture.

Still, the good heart and able brain were not content with their achievements, but continued to work and plan. Believing that industry would materially assist the farmers during the long, cold winters, Professor Sabsovich gradually but surely succeeded in interesting businessmen in his plans, and several factories were established. To these factories came workers of various trades in large numbers; they bought small homes, cultivated and developed the land around their homes, and, with thrift and diligence, rose to be prominent citizens of the colony.

It was then that the many-sided nature of the Professor had full play. As manager of the colony, he was at once brother and friend to each and every one of the colonists, rejoicing, encouraging, commending in good fortune; and consoling, cheering and sympathizing in misfortune and misery. He was also the peacemaker and arbitrator in all civic and domestic dissensions, wisely holding that Jewish cases should not come before the legal courts. In this way he prevented, or amicably settled, disputes that otherwise would have brought condemnation, or, to say the least, unfriendly criticism upon the colonists from the neighboring villagers, who were at first not disposed to regard them with favor.

As superintendent of the Woodbine Agricultural School, the Professor was a wise teacher and a judicious mentor. The boys found in him what many had in all their lives lacked—a source of inspiration and an interested friend and counselor. His rule was one of love, and as he sowed, so he reaped, for few fathers are as beloved and respected as the Professor is, even today, by many of his "boys."

Professor Sabsovich combined idealism with common sense and that he succeeded in bringing many of his dreams and visions to a very practical and material form amply attests that fact. For several years he cherished the hope of establishing in his beloved Woodbine a sort of Jewish government, under the state laws of New Jersey, and made every effort to incorporate Woodbine as a separate borough. Infinite patience and energy were required, yet, despite his manifold duties, the Professor ultimately succeeded in seeing his ardent desire fulfilled. Woodbine became a small Jewish government, a separate township, with its own Mayor, common council and its own city departments. In its gratitude, of course, Woodbine unanimously elected Professor Sabsovich its first Mayor, and its Mayor he continued until he was called to New York City to assume the responsibilities of general manager of the Baron de Hirsch Fund. This position he occupied until his death.

His last request was that he be buried in Woodbine—the Woodbine he made and loved, and which loved and will love him for all time. There he lies in peace, and, while his memory will remain green in the hundreds of hearts which knew and loved him, and the world continue to be enriched through the many lives he inspired and molded with his own indomitable spirit and high aspirations, his monument in real and tangible form will be the place where the immigrant Jew first learned the independence and blessing of living the life of a tiller of the soil—Woodbine.

Could any man desire a better monument?

The Baron de Hirsch Agricultural School
By Jacob G. Lipman

Director of New Jersey Agricultural School

IN planning the establishment of an agricultural colony the Trustees of the Baron de Hirsch Fund had occasion to examine and consider a number of sites. They finally selected a tract of about six thousand acres in the vicinity of Woodbine and Mount Pleasant in Cape May County, New Jersey. Their final decision as to the location was influenced partly by the low cost of the land and partly by the equable climate, favorable rainfall conditions and the proximity of the land to important eastern markets.

When Professor Sabsovich was appointed agricultural adviser of the newly established colony, and was later made responsible for its agricultural and industrial development, he realized that he was confronted by certain serious and almost insuperable difficulties. He recognized that the open, sandy and gravelly soils of Cape May have their possibilities. He saw that with proper methods of tillage and fertilization they could be made to grow profitable crops of vegetables, small fruits and tree fruits. He likewise recognized that the transforming of the newly cleared scrub oak and pine lands into productive soil called for a degree of technical skill and of special information not possessed by the immigrants from the fertile plains of southern Russia or the heavy, low, clay or loam soils of Poland and of the Baltic Provinces.

Gradually he came to feel that the first generation of farmers at Woodbine would, at best, make unsatisfactory progress, but that, by training the sons and daughters of these farmers in the newer methods of farming and particularly in those most directly applicable to the sandy and gravelly soils of the Coastal Plain, it might become possible to extend gradually the acreage of cleared and improved land and to place farming in the new colony on a sound basis. His conviction thus grew stronger in behalf of organizing more or less systematic training in technical and theoretical agriculture.

It is probable that the thought as to the organizing of an agricultural school at Woodbine was fairly mature in 1892. His contact with Dr. E. B. Voorhees, late Director of the New Jersey Experiment Station, apparently strengthened his determination to utilize to the fullest extent every opportunity that might offer itself in behalf of the establishment of an agricultural school. In the fall of 1893 he suggested to the writer of this article and to Jacob Kotinsky, another of the young farmers at Woodbine, that it might be wise for them to prepare themselves to enter the State Agricultural College at New Brunswick. His enthusiasm and his offer of moral and financial support served as a powerful stimulus to both of us, even though we had been out of school for some years. We applied ourselves faithfully to preparation in mathematics and in other subjects required for admission to the College.

Through the kindness of Professor Sabsovich we met Dr. Voorhees in the fall of 1893 and were by him further encouraged to prepare for an agricultural course at the College. His clear vision permitted Professor Sabsovich to see that the young men, through their contact with local needs and problems reinforced by a technical training in agriculture, might be made useful in supplying to their neighbors and to others who might become a part of the agricultural community the technical information so essential for the successful farming of the lighter soils of southern New Jersey. Throughout the fall of 1893 and the following spring and summer, Professor Sabsovich never missed an opportunity to encourage them in their preparation for college and to tell them of the opportunities for service that would open to them after they would have acquired the necessary training and preparation. He saw very clearly then that special problems of fertilization, special types of crops, the control of injurious insects and of fungus diseases, the feeding of livestock and many other problems were insistent and would become more insistent as time went on.

The Trustees of the Baron de Hirsch Fund, to whom Professor Sabsovich broached the subject of establishing an agricultural school, were not entirely ready to accept his suggestions. Not being as intimate as he was with the local conditions and needs, they could not see the connection between technical training and successful farming in Cape May County. In spite of lack of encouragement and in many instances of actual discouragement, Professor Sabsovich never lost faith in the ultimate success of his plan and urged whenever and wherever he could that funds be made available for systematic instruction in agriculture.

Finally a modest beginning was made in 1895, when instruction was more or less regularly organized for a group of the sons of local farmers. This instruction included classroom training in certain general subjects like arithmetic, modern history and geography, as well as purely agricultural subjects. The equipment was quite limited in extent. Nor were there funds available for the hiring of men trained in the teaching of technical agriculture. Indeed, the methods of teaching agriculture were quite crude in those days even at the state agricultural colleges. The body of knowledge, out of which textbooks are made, was meagre and the connection between classroom and laboratory instruction and field practice less clearly definite. For this reason, Professor Sabsovich and his associates had to feel their way as they went. Changes in the curriculum were made frequently as experience indicated improved methods of teaching. As funds became more ample, laboratory as well as classroom instruction was organized and the agricultural equipment was made more adequate.

Within a decade after the establishment of the school Professor Sabsovich succeeded, through untiring efforts, in providing a modem school plant. A large brick building, containing offices, classrooms and laboratories, dormitories large enough to house nearly one hundred students, dairy barns and silos, poultry buildings, greenhouses, storage sheds, machinery repair sheds, dining halls and other buildings were erected and courses in systematic study organized.

A body of young but promising instructors were gathered about Professor Sabsovich and the Baron de Hirsch Agricultural School became nearly two decades ago a pioneer in its field of vocational training in agriculture. Many of the faculty attained prominence as investigators and teachers in agriculture. Men like Professor White of Cornell, Lewis of Rutgers College, Billings of the United States Department of Agriculture, Garrigues of the Connecticut Agricultural College and a number of others began their professional careers at the Baron de Hirsch Agricultural School. The success of many of the graduates of the institution, their attainments in practical agriculture and in the profession of agriculture, bear testimony to Professor Sabsovich's clearness of vision and justified his faith and his devotion to the cause of agricultural education.

In later years the Trustees of the Baron de Hirsch Fund found it necessary to remove the agricultural school from Woodbine. They were guided principally by the wish to locate their school nearer to New York City, where most of the students came from and where a number of the active Trustees lived. There were also other reasons which to them seemed sufficient for building a new school plant in the vicinity of New York City. Meanwhile, the World War came to disturb the normal activities in the United States and the young men who would ordinarily have become students at the school were called to military service. The plan of the Trustees to develop a new school plant was, therefore, never carried out.

It is doubtful whether, under conditions as they exist today, there would be justification for making a large investment in the school in order that it might be made to function again. The vocational agricultural schools which have come into being within recent years make the reopening of the Baron de Hirsch Agricultural School unnecessary. It may be said, therefore, that Professor Sabsovich has established an institution which rendered an important service at a time when other institutions of a like nature were not available. He fulfilled a great public need. He laid the foundation of character; he taught many young men the power of ideals and of devoted service. Having for many years unselfishly labored for the cause, having been faithful to his trust, having built much that is indestructible, Professor Sabsovich needs no monument of granite to perpetuate his memory. His own example of loyal service will continue to be the inspiration of those who, like him, would serve their fellowmen.

The Jewish Farmers' Best Friend
By Joseph W. Pincus

PROFESSOR SABSOVICH was to me more than a teacher, an ideal preceptor. He was a real friend, who played a very determining part in my career, as he has played in that of many young men in America.

Even before I came to the United States I heard of Professor Sabsovich through the letters of my deceased father, who preceded me and the rest of our family to this country, by six or seven months. In the letters, my father wrote that he had had the pleasure of meeting Professor Sabsovich, a "landsman of ours from Berdiansk," and that, together with the Professor, just then appointed agriculturist by the newly organized Baron de Hirsch Fund of America, he had been inspecting farms in Bridgeton and other sections of the State of New Jersey.

Although I came to America in the fall of 1891, I did not have the opportunity of meeting Professor Sabsovich until the spring of 1895, when, largely on his advice, I entered the Baron de Hirsch Agricultural School at Woodbine. While the School was established in 1894, all the pupils up to 1895 were sons of Woodbine settlers, and I had the distinction of being the first student from outside the colony. Well do I remember the warm reception and hearty welcome which I received from the Professor and his family upon my arrival at Woodbine. From the first day of my acquaintance with him I formed an attachment for him which grew into real affection, increasing from year to year as I learned to know the man better and came into closer contact with him. It was entirely due to his advice and influence that I decided to enter an agricultural college, to return to Woodbine to become his co-worker and to devote twenty years of my life to work for and among Jewish farmers in the United States.

From the very beginning of the Woodbine Colony, while the tract of land was covered with pine and oak trees, which the pioneers were clearing away, he saw the necessity of imparting proper scientific information to the farmers. The first winter at Woodbine, Professor Sabsovich delivered lectures, illustrated with stereopticon slides, on agricultural topics. Notwithstanding his numerous and arduous duties at Woodbine, he found time to go frequently to the South Jersey Jewish colonies, at Alliance, Carmel and Norma, and address the farmers there, encourage them in their work, and deliver illustrated lectures. As far back as 1895 he advocated the establishment of a canning factory in these colonies, and about ten years later they were established in each one.

In 1894 he went to Chesterfield and Colchester, Connecticut, to deliver lectures to the Jewish farmers there. These were delivered in Yiddish. As Professor Sabsovich was born and reared in South Russia (Ukraine), and his native language was Russian, his Yiddish was rather poor, and he had to learn the language in order to make himself understood. The Professor was the first man in the United States to deliver lectures in Yiddish on agricultural topics, and he thus preceded by about fifteen years the work of itinerant instruction, and lecturing in Yiddish, inaugurated by the Jewish Agricultural and Industrial Society in 1908.

The first exhibition of farm products raised by Jewish farmers in America was also arranged by Professor Sabsovich in 1897 at the Hebrew Educational Society's building in Philadelphia. At this fair there were products not only from Woodbine, but also from all other Jewish colonies in New Jersey, as well as from many farmers in Connecticut. About five or six years later, also at the initiative of and participation in of Professor Sabsovich, an exhibition of Jewish life in the country was held at the Educational Alliance Building in New York City. This exhibit showed by photographs, charts, etc., how people lived on farms and in small villages in the United States. It was held under the auspices of the Baron de Hirsch Fund, the Jewish Agricultural Society, and the Removal Office, and was a revelation to city dwellers, as it revealed to them the fact that New York was not "America." There were hundreds of small villages and thousands of farms throughout the country where Jews lived happily, and where there was plenty of room and opportunity for city dwellers to breathe and live comfortably in beautiful surroundings, away from squalid and cramped quarters in the Big City. The exhibit was a wonderful success, and received the very favorable comment of the press. By special requests from Boston, Philadelphia and other large cities, it made the round of these places.

While talking of exhibits, it is also interesting to point out the fact that Professor Sabsovich was always interested in bringing to the attention of the outside world the ability of the Jew to become a successful farmer, and for this reason he never lost an opportunity of exhibiting the products and results of the work in Woodbine Colony. At many of the Cape May County Fairs and others held in the State of New Jersey, he encouraged the farmers and the Agricultural School to exhibit crops, and there was not a happier man in the State when a Jewish farmer or the School was awarded a prize or blue ribbon for a great pumpkin, a fine hen or a plate of superb peaches.

At the Universal Paris Exposition held in France in 1900 an exhibit was prepared under his direction, and a silver medal was given for the Exhibit of Special Education in Agriculture, another silver medal for Appliances and Methods in Horticulture and Arboriculture, and a grand prix for Exhibit of School Appliances.

At the Pan-American Exposition, held in Buffalo, N.Y., in 1901, for an exhibit of photographs, charts, etc., of Woodbine Colony and the Agricultural School, prepared by Professor Sabsovich, an Honorary Mention Diploma was awarded.

For the World's Fair, in St. Louis, Missouri, 1904, a more elaborate exhibit was prepared, consisting of several hundred photographs, showing in detail the, progress of the Colony in agricultural, social, religious and municipal fields, and also the work and life of the pupils at the Baron de Hirsch Agricultural School. Besides photographs there was a complete set of publications of the School, covering the Baron de Hirsch Fund, the Colony, pupils' work, textbooks used, charts, diagrams, reports, etc. The excellence of the exhibit can be judged not only by the award of the gold medal by the St. Louis Fair officials, but by the fact that Harvard University requested that this particular exhibit be presented to its Department of Social Science, where it is at present located.

All the time, during 1891 to 1905, although exceedingly occupied with the work of managing the Colony, and the organization and directing of the School, and notwithstanding several physical breakdowns suffered, Professor Sabsovich took an active interest in the welfare of the Jewish colonists in New Jersey and other states. He went frequently for conferences to New York with Mr. Arthur Reichow, in charge of the New York office, through whose efforts the sister organization, the Jewish Agricultural Industrial Society was started, and its first General Manager. This society took over all the agricultural work done by the Fund, with the exception of the Agricultural School. Later Professor Sabsovich was appointed a member of the Jewish Agricultural Society.

When Professor Sabsovich became the General Agent of the Baron de Hirsch Fund in 1906 and settled in New York City, his duties did not bring him into contact with the farmers, as this work had been taken over by the Jewish Agricultural Society. But many farmers, whenever they wanted a sympathetic hearing or advice on any subject, would write to him and frequently visit him, and he continued to take an active interest in the welfare of the Jewish farmers until his last days.

When the Federation of Jewish farmers of America was organized in January 1909, he was unanimously elected as the First Honorary member, and he addressed the first as well as all the other annual conventions. In the fall of 1909, in connection with the Convention of the Farmers, an agricultural fair and exhibit was held on the roof and in the gymnasium of the Educational Alliance, and Professor Sabsovich was chairman of the Jury of Awards. The fair was a very successful one and hundreds of exhibits of fruits, vegetables, dairy, grain products, and the results of the skill of the farmers' wives, in canned goods, preserves, etc., were sent in by Jewish farmers from New Jersey, Connecticut, New York, Massachusetts, and even from North Dakota and other western states. The Professor worked very hard for several days, examining all these offerings, with experts from the State Agricultural Experiment Stations, and awarding medals and diplomas for the best exhibits. Any reader happening to visit the homes of these farmers today would see these framed documents on the walls, where they would be pointed to with pride and the signature of Professor Sabsovich with sorrow.

On numerous occasions the Professor and I visited Colchester, Conn., Ellington, Conn., and Nassau, N.Y., to address the local associations of the Jewish farmers. I recollect that, on several occasions, although his health was very poor, he would go, in order that the farmers might not be disappointed, and frequently we had to travel fifteen to twenty miles by horses, as at that time there were no automobiles.

I remember clearly the last meeting attended by Professor Sabsovich. It was the organization meeting of the First Farmers' Saving and Loan Association under the newly organized Land Bank of New York, held at Centerville Station, Sullivan County, N. Y. It was early in the spring of 1914, and the Professor was convalescing after rather a severe illness at Cornwall-on-the-Hudson, and I stopped there for him, and he went, accompanied by Mrs. Sabsovich. We arrived safely at Centerville Station, and the Professor spoke a few encouraging words to the farmers. After the meeting we drove over to Mr. Samuel Shindler's farm at Hurleyville, and as the elevation is about fifteen hundred feet there and the air cold and rarefied to a marked degree, the Professor spent a very restless night. Mrs. Sabsovich was certainly glad to get him back home safely.

When the Federation of Jewish Farmers of America was organized, there was created an advisory committee, of which Professor Sabsovich, of course, was a member. He never missed a single meeting, unless ill in bed. He kept up this interest until the last days of his life. About a week or ten days before his death, Mr. Hein, President of the Federation of Jewish Farmers, and I visited him at his bedside, and he asked a number of questions about the work of the organization.

When the Jewish Agricultural Society started the publication of *The Jewish Farmer* in May 1908, I consulted with him on this venture, as I remembered that as far back as 1891 Professor Sabsovich was instrumental in publishing *The Jewish Farmer*; but, due to the rather limited number of Jewish farmers, it appeared for only about one year. He was, though, the first man in America who felt that there was a need for a special publication for them, and in 1904 he was editor of *Farmers' Leaflets*, published at Woodbine and containing timely articles on farming contributed by the instructors at the Agricultural School.

Besides his active participation in every phase of Jewish agriculture, Professor Sabsovich took an active part in the agricultural affairs of the state. He was for a number of years the Secretary of the Cape May County Board of Agriculture, and in that capacity submitted a number of very interesting reports on agricultural conditions in the County. These were all incorporated in the annual reports of the New Jersey State Board of Agriculture. Some of the contributions were so interesting and well written that the special attention of the Governor of New Jersey was called to them, and Professor Sabsovich was invited a number of times to important conferences. He was later appointed a Trustee of the New Jersey State Agricultural College and Experiment Station at New Brunswick, N. J., the first and probably the only Jew who ever held such an honorary position. He attended and took an active part in the annual conventions of the New Jersey State Board of Agriculture and the New Jersey State Horticultural Society.

There has not been an agricultural movement of any kind among Jews in which Professor Sabsovich did not participate, or regarding which his valued advice was not sought. Therefore, it is no wonder that all the old farmers in New Jersey and other eastern states remember and revere him. In Woodbine the clearing of the land, the planting of fruit trees, the equipment of the farms and all the numerous details were done under his personal supervision. He had a remarkable memory and could recall not only the names of all the farmers, but the names of all the children; and, when visiting the farms months, or even years later, would inquire about each and every individual member of the family.

Besides his remarkable influence on the Jewish farmer, I desire to note briefly his wonderful influence upon the younger generation. Early at the start of Woodbine Colony, he saw the importance, the necessity of interesting the children in farming, and it was largely due to his effort and perseverance that the trustees of the Baron de Hirsch Fund started the Agricultural School in 1895. The growth and progress of the School was largely due to his indomitable energy, courage and ability to work against almost insuperable difficulties and obstacles. I hope that someday a historian will be found to describe minutely the tremendous work that

Professor Sabsovich accomplished at the Woodbine Agricultural School. I wish to mention here the names of a few pioneer Jewish agriculturists who embarked on this career in 1894 and the years that followed, at a time when medicine was considered the only honorable profession for the Jew in America. It was largely, if not entirely, due to the Professor's advice and frequently to the financial aid obtained by him for many of the students at the agricultural colleges that so many of the men took up these courses.

The first men who were graduated from agricultural colleges in the United States in 1898 were: Jacob G. Lipman, Jacob Kotinsky and myself. Dr. Jacob G. Lipman, besides becoming a renowned soil bacteriologist and author of several scientific books, is now Director of the New Jersey State Agricultural Experiment Station and Dean of the College of Agriculture of New Jersey State University, the highest agricultural educative position ever held by a Jew in America, or probably in the world. Jacob Kotinsky was for a number of years a prominent entomologist, occupying positions of responsibility in the Hawaiian Islands and in the U. S. Department of Agriculture.

Among many others, the following may be mentioned: David Fink, entomologist in the U. S. Department of Agriculture; Marcus Smulyan, also an entomologist; Dr. Charles B. Lipman, Professor of Soil Chemistry at the University of California; George W. Simon, Western Agent of the Jewish Agricultural Society; Dr. Arthur Goldhaft, a successful practicing veterinarian at Vineland, N. J.; Dr. I. V. Stone, a chemist. I could go on and enumerate many, many more successful farmers, doctors, veterinarians, social workers, lawyers, etc., who owe their start in life in this—their new country of adoption—to the advice, help and splendid example of service, for the benefit of his people, of their dear friend and teacher, Professor H. L. Sabsovich.

The foregoing brief sketch of the Professor's devotion and activity for the Jewish farmer is very inadequate, and does not do justice to the first man who had the real vision that in farming lies the salvation and regeneration of the Jewish race. Had his advice been followed to a larger degree and had there been more dreamers of his kind, we might have had a different picture of the Jew in America and less suffering in the whole world! Had we now a few hundred thousands, instead of a few thousands of successful Jewish farmers in the United States, possibly we would not have restriction of immigration and vast numbers of our unfortunate brethren in Central Europe would have a haven of refuge! Had we several hundreds of successful colonies and several good agricultural schools, the prospects for the Jew in America and the ultimate Jewish settlement of Palestine would be much brighter!

The hundreds of young men who have been graduated from the agricultural schools and colleges in this country, and many hundreds who are now students at these institutions still have an opportunity to show to the world that Professor Sabsovich, the pioneer agriculturist and dreamer, did not sacrifice his life in vain; that his wonderful example of devotion to the cause of the Jew in agriculture has not been lost; and that coming years will show how successful the settlements in Palestine will be and how multiplied in prosperity and numbers the Jewish farmers of America.

The Leader of Jewish Agriculture in America

By George W. Simon

THE historian recording the progress of Jewish Farming in the United States, would undoubtedly consider
the late Professor H. L. Sabsovich as the father of the
organized Jewish agricultural movement in the United
States. While there were several attempts to colonize the
Jewish people prior to 1890, the leaders were, as a rule,
laymen and knew little about agriculture. Their work had
mainly a charitable aspect with a touch of idealism to it,
and therefore the results were usually negative. Professor
Sabsovich was the first trained agriculturist connected
with the Jewish farming movement in this country, and
his were the first efforts of a systematic and practical
nature towards creating a Jewish farming class in the
United States. He had great faith in the possibilities of
Jewish farming in this country and possessed a keen
insight as to how to develop the new field of activities
among our Jewish people.

The general public at large heaped considerable
criticism upon the Professor in the Jewish press and
because the Baron de Hirsch Fund concentrated its

efforts in Woodbine, New Jersey, in the early nineties, a locality which was in the poorest agricultural section of that state. It was natural for outsiders to blame the man who was at the head of that enterprise. Had the people considered the matter carefully, they would have learned that the Professor was not responsible for the selection of the locality. They would then have realized the heroic and indefatigable work of a great leader who sacrificed his life and health to make a success of the enterprise in spite of the adverse conditions. They would have appreciated his efforts to further the cause of Jewish farming and thus protect the name of our Jewish people by proving to the world at large that the Jews can be producers as well as consumers.

While I lived in New York, it was my privilege to spend Saturdays and Sundays with the late Professor Sabsovich and take long walks through the parks, when we would discuss various problems pertaining to the question of Jewish farming. About three years before he passed away, during one of these conversations, he told me, that in looking over the old papers in the office, he came across his first report which he submitted after his first visit to Woodbine. In that report he pointed out the difficulties which must be overcome in Woodbine and the natural obstacles in the way of success. He then suggested that the Jewish settlers should be directed to New England, where land with good buildings could be purchased very reasonably, and where the conditions are more favorable to diversified farming. A few years later his suggestion was adopted and since then the efforts of the Fund were directed towards settling people on developed farms in New England, New York, New Jersey and elsewhere. It is a most gratifying fact that the most progressive and prosperous settlement of Jewish farmers in the United States is located in Connecticut, where they practically control the tobacco growing industry.

Nevertheless, Professor Sabsovich's work in Woodbine has not been done in vain, since it will serve for the future leaders in the agricultural movement as a lighthouse serves to the stranded ship in the night or in the fog, warning them to keep away from the shore and look out for the breakers. The experiments carried on in Woodbine, N. J., while not always bringing the desired results, are nevertheless invaluable and will serve as a basis for practical study of land settlements and will save a loss of time and money, as well as prevent failure, if the people who are interested will avail themselves of the opportunity to look into this carefully. In his work at the Baron de Hirsch Agricultural School, which is discussed elsewhere, he has helped to create a class of trained scientific Jewish agriculturists, whose leadership is indispensable to the cause of Jewish farming. Many of these have become leaders in agriculture in the United States.

During the last ten years of his life as the head of the Baron de Hirsch Fund, his activities were in widely scattered fields of social endeavor, but his influence upon the agricultural movement among the Jewish people, while indirect, was nevertheless predominant.

Professor Sabsovich was one of the first to advocate and edit *The Jewish Farmer* publication in Yiddish in the year 1900, which was later on suspended for a while until we had sufficient people who could utilize the services of such a paper. He was one of the first to advocate the introduction of horticulture and agriculture in the various orphan asylums in the United States, since in his opinion many of the wards would develop an inclination to take farming up as a vocation and thus afford many a healthy opportunity to grow outside of the congested and overcrowded cities. The importance of this suggestion has not been realized as yet, but the fact is that while we have gradually developed a class of Jewish farmers and while we have a number of young men who have taken up agriculture as a vocation from the practical and scientific point of view, most of them are handicapped in carrying out their desire because they cannot find Jewish girls who would be willing to share with them their lives on a farm. We are still to find a way to develop the love for country life among our Jewish women. The suggestion made by the late Professor Sabsovich would serve as a good nucleus for that purpose.

For twenty-five years, quietly and unassumingly he continued to use his influence in directing the agricultural movement among our Jewish people in the United States, and the results obtained in that field can to a great extent be placed to his credit, since the majority of the present leaders in that field have directly or indirectly felt his influence.

Unfortunately, like Moses, he was not destined by fate to lead his people to the Promised Land. He did not live to see the present development of the Jewish agricultural movement in this country, which is now greatly expanding. There were very few Jewish farmers when Professor Sabsovich first started to work among our people and encourage them to take up farming.

There are now over 10,000 prosperous Jewish farmers in the United States, tilling and occupying over 1,000,000 acres of land worth from $75,000,000 to $100,000,000 at the least. I am sure that he would rejoice to witness the splendid progress attained by our Jewish people in the field of farming, but I am inclined to believe that he had the foresight to feel it and to know it, which gave him the courage to continue persistently his fight in that direction.

The writer, who has for the past fifteen years been actively connected with the Jewish farming movement in the United States, is in a position to state authoritatively that the Jewish farmers are recognized as leaders in their various communities. Furthermore, in some branches of farming, such as tobacco growing, fruit growing, poultry raising, and other branches, our Jewish farmers, if they do not excel, are at least equal to any of the native farmers in the United States.

In the above brief sketch I endeavored modestly to pay a well deserved tribute to a great man, a leader of our people, who sacrificed his life in his efforts to serve a worthy cause. May his life serve as an inspiration to the Jewish people and especially to those who are engaged in the field of social endeavor, so we can at least say that the Professor did not live in vain.

Afterword
By Rosemary Reidy
Stockton Class of '20

Over a century ago, Katherine Sabsovich was riding a train to New York, reflecting on the life of her deceased husband, when the words of George Herbert echoed in her mind, "Only the actions of the just smell sweet and blossom in the dust." In this brief afterword, a twenty-first century student and editor recalls her own reading of *Adventures in Idealism* and thinks of Herbert's words as she, too, reflects on the life of H. L. Sabsovich.

In this loving biography, Katherine Sabsovich details the impact that one gifted Jewish immigrant had on the community of Woodbine, New Jersey, and the wider Jewish community in America. Professor Sabsovich, as he was addressed in life, brought agriculture, education and community to the small rural town of Woodbine during the late nineteenth and early twentieth centuries. Under his guidance and care, it grew to be a well-known destination near the Jersey shore, attracting travelers far and wide; it became a leading site for agricultural research and innovation. Known for his down-to-earth spirit, his common sense, and especially his honest character, Sabsovich dedicated his life to creating solutions to difficulties encountered by Jewish immigrants.

Katherine Sabsovich's love and devotion to her late husband is abundantly clear throughout the work. She notes the happy times, the triumphs and the struggles. Sabsovich had a life-long susceptibility to illness, and his interactions with Woodbine residents were often challenging. Despite this, he left behind a legacy of fair-mindedness and forward-looking problem solving. Professor Sabsovich set out to reintroduce the Jewish population to their agricultural heritage and to do so with the most up-to-date methods and science. He was able successfully to aid not only recent immigrants, but the entire Jewish American community and, indeed, all Americans.

The character of H. L. Sabsovich is his most attractive quality. He was kind, and just and compulsively trustworthy. He worked incessantly to build community and correct social ills where he could. His patriotism, which flowed from opportunities offered by his adopted homeland, was often on display. His is an inspiring story.

Additional Illustrations, new to this edition

(Courtesy of the Paul W. Schopp Collection)

Adventures in Idealism

Baron de Hirsch Agricultural School, Woodbine, N. J., c. 1910

A Ploughing Contest, Baron de Hirsch Agricultural School, Woodbine, N. J., c. 1910

School Building, Woodbine, N. J., c. 1910

Public School No. 2, Woodbine, N. J., c. 1910

Fire Department, Woodbine, N. J., c. 1910

Hotel Rosenfeld, Woodbine, N. J., c. 1910

Machine Shop of M. L. Bayard & Co., Woodbine, N. J., c. 1917

The Woodbine Children's Clothing Co., Woodbine, N. J., c. 1910

Residence of Joseph Rabinovich, Woodbine, N. J., c. 1910

Woodbine Brotherhood Synagogue, Woodbine, N. J., c. 1910

View of Washington Ave., Woodbine, N. J., c. 1910

Real photo postcard of School Building, Woodbine, N. J., c. 1906

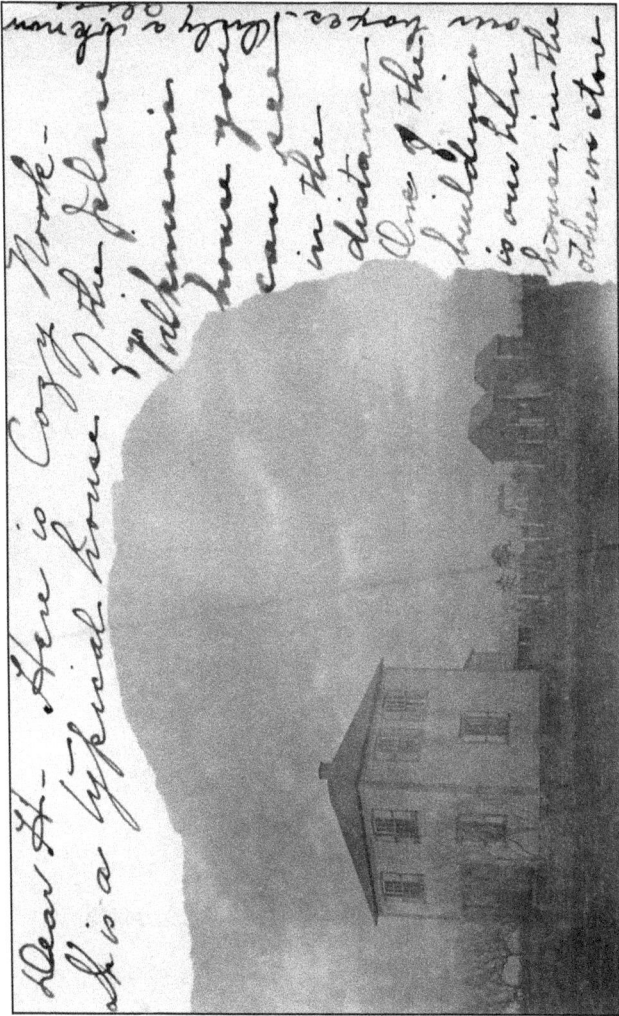

Real photo postcard, a Woodbine farm, Woodbine, N. J., c. 1906

Index

Colophon

The editing and design of *Adventures in Idealism* was a team effort by editing interns at Stockton University. Angela Capella, Kailey Romero and Josh Champlin established the initial typesetting. Mariana Isabel Ramos Arias and Samantha Brown designed the preliminary layout, which Kailey Romero refined. Sarah Augustine, Brad Bacchetti, Jack Kahvejian, Nicholas Miele, and Somaillan Slack proofread sections of the text. Rosemary Reidy completed the final proofreading and wrote the Afterword. Tom Kinsella supervised publication.

We thank Mark Demitroff for his suggestion that we republish this title. And, and of course, thanks to Jane Stark for her foreword.

Text font is 12-point Baskerville; quotations are 11-point Baskerville.

www.ingramcontent.com/pod-product-compliance
Lightning Source LLC
Chambersburg PA
CBHW031828090426
42741CB00005B/167